Healing Discourses in the Gospel of Mark

Healing Discourses in the Gospel of Mark

A Socio-Political Reading

Arun Thomas

Christian World Imprints

First Published in 2020 by

Christian World Imprints
Christian Publishing & Books from India
C-3, Wazirpur Industrial Area, **Delhi-110052**
cwidelhi2017@gmail.com
www.ChristianWorldImprints.com
Phone: +91 11 41526079

ISBN: 978-93-5148-419-6

Printed in India.

Dedicated to the loving memory of
My father
Thomas K. Abraham

Contents

Foreword

The Bible, as the word of God, surprises us by the fact that the newer approaches to the bible brings forth newer dimensions of the text. In the 21st century Biblical and theological researches propose new horizons of the text using interdisciplinary methodologies, especially that of the social sciences. Critical Discourse Analysis is one of such methodological searches for the new meaning and exploration of truth. Critical Discourse Analysis is used to understand society on the basis of language. This analysis emphasises that ideas, facts and knowledge are not static, but change as the discourse(s) change.

There are numerous ways to study the healing stories in the New Testament. But, a focused attempt to study on the healing stories recorded in the Gospel according to Mark, through the methodological framework of Critical Discourse Analysis is a rare attempt. In this book Rev. Arun Thomas Abraham, has delineated such a study on the healing stories in the Gospel according to Mark, using the methodology of Critical Discourse Analysis. Therefore, this study deserves our attention and appreciation.

This book depicts a new set of reflections on the healing stories. The study helps us to identify healing stories beyond the familiar understanding of the miracles performed by Jesus Christ, finding out 'healing' as a socio – political discourse. The book tries to divulge how Jesus uses Healing Discourses as a tool for change and transformation of the social – political – religious space. Another important aspect of this study is considering the healing stories as a discourse, which carries multiple dialogues, questions and answers. The healing discourse opens the opportunity to bring many voices of the text and context into conversation. Therefore, the healing stories could be seen not a monologue rather a discourse. Critical Discourse Analysis also brings together the discursive and critical approaches to religion, both of which have been underrepresented in the current mainstream Indian theological scholarship.

I appreciate Rev. Arun Thomas Abraham for his effort in writing this book. I wish and pray that this book may invite the students of theology, literature, sociology of religion and anyone who is interested in the deeper search of religion to engage with the method and emulate the wisdom shared in this book.

With prayers and blessing

Dr. Joseph Mar Thoma Metropolitan
Poolatheen, Thiruvalla

Acknowledgements

The task of this research would not have been accomplished without the support, encouragement and generosity of many persons, who have stood with me in every step of my academic expedition. I am grateful to all of them. I thank God Almighty who has called me, and strengthened me with ever abounding grace in my weakness and enabled me for His ministry. This monograph is an extension of my thesis during the Bachelor of Divinity Studies at the United Theological College, Bangalore. My thanks are due to Mar Thoma Church for providing me with the opportunity to be a part of the great legacy called 'The United Theological College', Bangalore.

I express my sincere gratitude to my esteemed teacher and guide Rev. Dr. C. I David Joy who has become the wind under my wings; who has guided me, challenged my thoughts and inspired me to expand the horizons of the expedition. I thank him of the profound introduction for this book.

I am grateful to my mentor during my theological education Most. Rev. Dr. Joseph Mar Thoma Metropolitan for his blessings and support. I thank The Mar Thoma Metropolitan for the meaningful forward note for this book. I reserve my gratitude to my beloved teachers in UTC who motivated me throughout my academic journey.

Indeed I am grateful to the administration and the staff of the Libraries at United Theological College, Bangalore, Mar Thoma Theological Seminary, Kottayam, T.M.A.M. Research and Orientation Center Kottayam, for their friendly support.

I am ever grateful for the love and guidance of my dear brother Rev. Sam T. Koshy, Resaerch Scholar at University of Bern, Switzerland, for his continuing academic companionship which truly inspires and encourages me in the journey of learning.

I also extend my sincere gratitude to Dr. P. M. Girish, my teacher and a well known linguist and Head of the Department of Malayalam, University of Madras, who introduced Critical Discourse Analysis and encourage me to reflect on the academic possibilities of this methodology in religious studies. His continuing love and wisdom is a true source of inspiration.

My love and gratitude goes to dear Sudhanshu Kanda and Christian World Imprints, New Delhi for accepting this research for publication. Mr. Sudhanshu's effort and wisdom in bringing out Christian literature through CWI is a remarkable contribution to the Biblical academia.

Finally, I want to thank my family for their love and support. My parents, Lt. Thomas K. Abraham and Annie Thomas, Varghese K. Daniel and Rajamma Varghese, for their sacrificial love and encouragement for my studies and writing. I am also deeply obliged to Sumi, my wife, who has been a constant source of support and encouragement throughout the writing. My love to Adiv, our son, for his innocent smile and charm, which motivate me again and again. This book is dedicated to the evergreen memories of my dear Achachen, Lt. Thomas K. Abraham.

Introduction

Rev. Arun Thomas has written a beautiful interpretation of the scripture by applying Critical Discourse Analysis. He critically evaluated the healing stories in mark 2:1-12, mark 5:1-12 and mark 10:46-52 in the light of Critical Discourse Analysis. By exposing the genre and social location on marken text, Rev. Arun Thomas was able to propose a new hermenutical paradigm for studying the text. In todays context a proper and possible exposition of Bible is mandatory as the people of God encounter many issues of faith. Anthony C. Thiselten, a pioneer of biblical hermeneutics considers 'hermeneutics provides exposition and critical discussions of hermeneutics as a multidisciplinary area". It is important to note that only through interactive and multidisciplinary approaches; one can enter into this world of biblical hermeneutics.

Critical Discourse Analysis is a critical study of the text by keeping the tension and struggle reflected in the text. This analysis takes linguistic and psycho-social approaches one step further by analysing the data from a decidedly critical stance. This Analysis examines the dominant and subordinate discourses on offer in society and explores notions of resistance and appropriation of discourses among various social actors. In doing so discourse analysis not only captures something important about the social world, but also plays a key ethical and political role in showing how social phenomena are discursively constituted: it demonstrates how things come to be as they are, that they could be different, and thereby that they can be changed. For Critical Discourse Analysis, every discourse is a product of a social context. The work of Michel Foucault, for example, has been particularly influential in Critical Discourse Analysis. In The Archaeology of Knowledge, Foucault posited that for words and concepts that we assume have real, distinct referents, we must relate "them to the body of rules that enable them to form as objects of a discourse and thus constitute the conditions of their historical appearance" (Foucault, 2000, p. 427). This 'body of rules' leads to the formation of dominant discourses, or texts whose authority permits their passing as knowledge, truth, immutable law, or 'commonsense'. Critical Discourse Analysis emphasises that ideas, facts and knowledge are not static, but change as the discourse(s) change.

By analysing the marken text, specifically the healing miracle stories Rev. Arun Thomas has shown his brilliancy in exploring this tension and struggle in the text. I am sure his work is a welcome addition to the field of New Testament Hermenutics. I appreciate Rev. Arun Thomas for using his critical faculty and faith commitment in studying the text. I whole heartedly present this book and recommend the readers to engage in a meaningful conversation with the text.

Rev. Dr. C. I. David Joy
Principal, KUTC Trivandrum

Chapter 1

Critical Discourse Analysis
Theory and Approaches

1.1. Introduction

Critical Discourse Analysis seeks to reinvigorate any given text, investigating its discursive sources and attempting to cover and reimagine those sources of power, dominance, disparity, and bias under the contextual references of particular social, political, and historical spheres. Hence this methodology of Critical Discourse Analysis (CDA) is an unveiling of the text in relation to its backdrop which acts as an influential source for its form, content and meaning. The role of power and other factors in socio-political-cultural and religious contexts is the key ultimatum from where the texts ceaselessly derive their meaning and form and get shaped. CDA does better in picking out the cues and piecing them together to arrive at the meaningful frame of the text. This chapter is an attempt to discuss the methodological frame and brief historical development of the Critical Discourse Analysis.

The discussion overviews important paradigm shifts that took place in the methodology of Critical Discourse Analysis with exploring some important scholars and their contributions in this field of study.

1.2. Discourse

Meaning and content of the word discourse will undergo changes according to the time and methodologies. The term discourse could be defined succinctly as the meaning of an oral or written narrative.[1] The theory of CDA exploits the term 'discourse' in two dimensions-as an abstract noun and as a concrete countable noun. Discourse taken as an abstract noun, locates language in use as a social practice with a demanding stress on traits such as paragraphs, utterances, whole texts or genre; the other way, considered as a concrete countable noun leads to a 'practice not just of representing the world, but of signifying the world, constituting and constructing the world in meaning.'[2] Hodge and Kress give a distinct understanding of variations among message, text and discourse. The minimal unit of the semiotic form, the message is featured with a 'source and a goal, a social context and purpose' when juxtaposed with larger units such as texts and discourses.

The writers distinguish between these in defining a 'text' as a structure of message or message traces which has a socially ascribed unity and a 'discourse' as the social process in which texts are embedded. Texts, they emphasize, have their place in a social system of signs that is dynamic. Therefore, texts are both the material realization of systems of signs, and also the site where change continually takes place.[3]

---

[1] Teun A. Van Dijk, *Discourse and Power* (New York: Palgrave Macmillan, 2008), 8.

[2] Norman Fairclough, *Discourse and Social Change* (Cambridge: Polity Press, 1992), 64.

[3] R. Hodge and G Kress. *Social Semiotics* (Cambridge: Polity Press, 1988), 5-6.

The post enlightenment era also played an important role in bringing the methodological shift in the critical discourse analysis. The postmodern ideologies created major changes in the theological epistemology. It proposed the end of metanarratives. A metanarrative is a grand narrative, as it silences the stories of the weak and marginalized and imposes those of the strong and powerful.[4] For postmodernism discourses are parts of the little narratives. The postmodernist shift tried to use discourses as the counter movements against the mega narratives. Therefore, discourses carry an alternative for the wisdom that the enlightment modernity proposed. It questioned the myth of the unitary subject, idea of abstract universality, the quest for the ultimate foundations of rationality, and the essentialist conception of the social totality. Postmodern discourse theory suggests the abandon of the discourse of the universal and recognises the particularity of all claims to knowledge and truth. Critical Discourse analysis also carries the task of developing little narratives in order to make alternative reading.

1.3. Critical Discourse Analysis

Both the terms Critical Linguistics (CL) and Critical Discourse Analysis (CDA) are often supplanted for one another. Earlier nomenclature of the theory, CL has been found to be wanting, paving way for the theorists to shift it to CDA in recent times. Hence the preference for the term CDA in this thesis. The ideological roots and base of CDA are embedded with different other disciplines such as Literary Studies, Philosophy, Socio-Psychology, Cognitive Science, Text linguistics, Rhetorics, Sociolinguistics, as well as in Applied Linguistics, Anthropology, and Pragmatics. Language is at the core of critical discourse analysis.[5] Critical Discourse Analysis acknowledges meaning as a parameter constructed socially wherein language and other sign

---

[4] Steven Connor "Introduction" in *The Cambridge Companion to Postmodernism* ed. Steven Connor (UK: Cambridge University Press, 2004), 15.

[5] Terry Locke. *Critical Discourse Analysis* (New York: Continuum, 2004), 11.

systems have contributed to its wholesome construction through their mediations.

1.3.1. Evaluation of CDA

Few linguists and literary theorists at the University of East Anglia, framed this theory of Critical Linguistics in the late 1970s. Halliday's Systematic Functional Linguistics (SFL) was the base upon which their approach rested. CL practitioners such as Trew viewed the possibility of "isolating ideology in discourse" and showing "how ideology and ideological processes are manifested as systems of linguistic characteristics and processes." His aim saw the development of CL's analytical tools based on SFL.[6]

Ideational, inter personal, and textual functions are the three operational categories of functions performed simultaneously by language in use according to the CL practitioners as they have been trailing behind the theory of Halliday. According to Fowler and Fairclough on the one hand the ideational function marks the experiences of the speakers in lieu of the world and its phenomena, on the other hand, the interpersonal function represents the extracts of speakers' own attitudes and evaluations about the phenomena in question, and establishing a relationship between speakers and listeners.[7] The textual function corroborates the functioning of ideational and interpersonal factors. It is through the textual function of language that speakers are able to produce texts that are understood by listeners. It has the liaising function of bridging the discourse to the co-text and con-text in which it occurs.

Majority of the CDA theorists endorse language as a 'social act', generally attributed to Halliday's view.[8] According to Fowler CL, shares a common trait with sociolinguistics, as

---

[6] Roger Fower, *Literature as Social Discourse: The Practice of Linguistic Criticism* (USA: Indiana University Press, 1981), 23.

[7] Norman, Fairclough, *Critical Discourse Analysis* (Boston: Addison Wesley, 1995), 25.

[8] Chouliaraki, Lilie and Norman Fairclough. *Discourse in Late Modernity – Rethinking Critical Discourse Analysis* (Edinburgh: Edinburgh University Press, 1999), 54.

it also asserts that, "there are strong and pervasive connections between linguistic structure and social structure."[9] However, whereas in sociolinguistics "the concepts 'language' and society are divided…so that one is forced to talk of links between the two, for CL language is an integral part of social process."[10]

CDA and SFL make certain assumptions central to language spoken by speakers: choices in vocabulary and grammar made by speakers are consciously and unconsciously "principled and systematic."[11] Thus choices are ideologically based. According to Fower the "relation between form and content is not arbitrary or conventional, but......form signifies content."[12] Encapsulating the approach is the main idea that language is a social act.

1.3.2. Further Development of CDA

CL and its more recent referent, CDA, have expanded its base. The expansions have led to certain deliberations upon few of the concerns and misgivings with earlier versions of CL. The first concern was related to the role of the audiences and their possible interpretations of discourse which gear towards the different direction from that of the discourse analysts. The second aspect views to widen the scope of analysis beyond the textual, extending it to the intertextual analysis.[13]

Both concerns have been looked into by Fairclough. He claims that the earliest work in CL did not adequately focus on the "interpretive practices of audiences."[14] The earlier approach of CL had a notion that the interpretations of the audience and analysts are similar. In the same light, commenting on Fowler, Boyd-Barrett's statement that there is a tendency towards the classic fallacy of attributing particular 'readings' to readers, or

---

[9] Roger Fower, *Language and Control (London: Routledge, 1979),*185.

[10] Roger Fower, *Language and Control,* 189.

[11] Roger Fower, *Language and Control,* 188.

[12] Roger Fower, *Language and Control,* 188.

[13] Chouliaraki, Lilie and Norman Fairclough. *Discourse in Late Modernity – Rethinking Critical Discourse Analysis*, 73.

[14] Norman, Fairclough, *Critical Discourse Analysis*, 37.

media 'effects,' solely on the basis of textual analysis has also to be taken into consideration.

Fairclough maintains that earlier contributions in CL had a thorough dealing with their grammatical and lexical analysis whereas the intertextual analyses of texts were not keyed in with a larger attention: "the linguistic analysis is very much focused upon clauses, with little attention to higher-level organization properties of whole texts."[15] He insists that "mention of these limitations is not meant to minimize the achievement of critical linguistics they largely reflect shifts of focus and developments of theory in the past twenty years or so."[16] The shifts of focus and developments of theory as Fairclough reiterates on, do not lead consequentially in the creation of a single theoretical framework. CDA in the light of modern approach, according to Bell & Garret, "is best viewed as a shared perspective encompassing a range of approaches rather than as just one school."[17] Also, van Dijk remarks that CDA is not a specific direction of research hence it does not have a unitary theoretical framework. In spite of that, van Dijk follows on, "given the common perspective and the general aims of CDA, we may also find overall conceptual and theoretical frameworks that are closely related."[18]

1.4. Theories and Approaches

1.4.1. Michael Foucault

For Michael Foucault, discourse is a specific way of communication. His monograph 'Archaeology of Knowledge' dwelled on this thought in detail. He defines discourse as a statement in which the knowledge takes its form. Knowledge and power have a confrontation in the wide space of discourse. Foucault's concept of power was one of the important

[15] Norman, Fairclough, *Critical Discourse Analysis*, 28.

[16] Norman, Fairclough, *Critical Discourse Analysis*, 28.

[17] Allen Bell and P. Garrett. *Approches to Media Discourse* (UK: Wiley-Blackwell,1998), 7.

[18] Allen Bell and P. Garrett. *Approches to Media Discourse* (UK: Wiley-Blackwell, 1998), 27.

methodological tools for CDA. According to Foucault power is not a 'thing, or a capacity', which can be owned either by State, social class or particular individual. Instead it is relation between different individuals and groups and only exists when it is being exercised.[19] Hence, human relationships are primarily compared to institutions and governments. Moreover power reaches into the very grain of individuals, touches their bodies and inserts itself into their actions and attitudes, their discourses, learning processes and everyday lives.[20]

Foucault conceptualizes power as a productive force which is extant across the world among all the individuals and hence he brings it as a universal phenomenon. But, Foucault is also aware of the fact that human order and their frontiers are supple to limitations and so he does not attempt to clinch any universal structure or system for power.

Foucault believed in 'order'[21] and he also viewed every existing order in knowledge, society, and culture as limited and that needs to be challenged from time to time. Without being challenged, it may abet injustice and ignorance. Thus, Foucault foregrounds social justice as a crucial and ethical consideration that requires keen attention, examination and action. CDS also tries to incorporate this aspect in the methodology thus, the analysis of the discourses may reflect the alternative justice and models of change which the discourse produces.

Foucault rubbishes power when it is identified with the quantitative/inherent and fixed notions. Nothing is excluded out by power. For him every social interaction is power relations ('force relation').[22] Power is not an institution, and not a

---

[19] See Clare O'Farrell, *Michel Foucault* (New Delhi: Sage Publication, 2005), 99.

[20] Michel Foucault, *Discipline and Punish* (New York: Vintage Book, 1979), 30.

[21] He believed that the order of co-existence is present both within culture as well as in the physical world.

[22] Mothy Varkey, *Concept of Power in Sermon on the Mount* (Tiruvalla: CSS, 2010), 18.

structure; neither is it a certain strength we are endowed with; it is the name that one attributes to a complex strategic situation in a particular society.[23] Power is therefore, distinct from authority. "The exercise of power is not simply a relationship between two partners, individual or collective; it is a way in which some act on others."[24] Power is dormant until it is exercised by few on others. Hence, it can be validated that power becomes an act of few over others' actions.

Foucault critiques violence as it has a tendency to shut down all possibilities and nullify the other end with passivity. On the contrary, power provides one with the opportunities of opening up with inventions. Though it cannot be claimed that power relations are totally devoid of violence, its basic nature is not constituted with the principle of violence. Therefore, power is a set of actions on possible actions. Various rudiments make sure that they govern the smooth functioning of power. It is viewed not as a commodity but in terms of relationality. It is also not considered as a possession or capacity of groups or an individual.[25]

It is not too simple a body to be obtained or held easily. It should be viewed as flow which runs through the whole social body, functions in the form of a chain and its existence is based on the exercise of productive network which are spread everywhere and in which all are caught.[26] The Foucaultian analysis begins from the micro-level. It is impossible for knowledge not to engender power.[27] It is knowledge that sets apart 'the other' and 'freezes the other' and exercises power over them. Power could be credited with the productivity of domains of objects and rituals

---

[23] Michel Foucault, *History of Sexuality*, vol. 1 (New York: Random House, 1990), 93.

[24] Michel Foucault, *Power*, ed. James D. Faubion (USA: New Press, 1994), 340.

[25] See Michael Foucault, *Discipline and Punish* (New York: Vintage Books, 1979), 98.

[26] Michael Foucault, *Discipline and Punish*, 61.

[27] M. Sarup, *An Introductory Guide to Post-structuralism and Postmodernism* (New York: Harvester Wheatsheaf, 1993), 74.

of truth.[28] Power has under its grip, various strategies, and one among them is discipline. Surveillance or hierarchical observation to be enabled, normalising judgement and examinations will be established as part of power of power mechanism. The devices of power namely correction, gratification and punishment are not promoters of individualism, as a popular misconception is in vogue. They rather fabricate the individuals.

1.4.2. Van Dijk: Socio-cognitive Model

Van Dijk is one of the most influential figures in critical studies of media discourse, as his breakthrough ideologies of CDA embrace even the fields that do not necessarily fit within the CDA perspective

Van Dijk applied the theory of discourse analysis to media texts mainly focusing on the representation of ethnic groups and minorities in Europe. His News Analysis (1988) incorporates his general theory of discourse to the discourse of news in the press, and applies the theory to authentic texts of news reports at both the national and international level. Unlike others, van Dijk pitches in for a thorough analysis of either the textual and structural level of media discourse and analysis and also explanations at the production and "reception" or comprehension level.[29] It distinguishes him from other news discourse analysts.

Van Dijk proposed the analysis of "structures at various levels of description" which embedded within itself not only the grammatical, phonological, morphological and semantic level but also "higher level properties" such as coherence, overall themes and topics of news stories and the whole schematic forms and rhetorical dimensions of texts. But, he felt the inadequacy of the structural analysis for Discourse is not just an isolated textual or dialogic structure; it is a complex web of communicative event enjoined to it which also embodies a social context, featuring participants (and their properties) as well as production and

[28] Michael Foucault, *Discipline and Punish*, 94.

[29] Teun A. Van Dijk, *Discourse and Power*, 41.

reception processes.[30] Van Dijk's analysis was remarkable in the way that it emphasized on 'production processes' which is nothing but the journalistic and institutional practices of news – making and the economic and social practices. These production processes, he reiterates, can shape the way of the creation of media discourse and also could be overtly related to the structures of media discourse.

The other strand of attention given to "reception processes", is the engagement of considering the comprehension, "memorization and reproduction" of news information. Van Dijk's effort to analyse media is to underline the relationships among the three levels of news text production (structure, production and comprehension processes) and their relationship with the wider social context they are embedded within. To make those relationships identifiable and credible, van Dijk's analysis is dealt with at two levels: microstructure and macrostructure.

The semantic relations between propositions, syntactic, lexical and other rhetorical elements which contribute to the coherent structure of the text, and quotations, direct or indirect reporting that avails to the factuality to the news report are all the features which van Dijk focused at the microstructure level examination.

Sociocognition-social and personal cognition welded together-bridges society and discourse. Van Dijk defines social cognition as "the system of mental representations and processes of group members."[31] To him, ideologies "are the overall, abstract mental systems that organize … socially shared attitudes" that "indirectly influence the personal cognition of group members."[32] He calls the mental representations of individuals that pattern in such social actions and interactions as models which "control how people act, speak or write or how they understand the social practices of others". Mental representations "are often articulated

---

[30] Teun A. Van Dijk, *Handbook of Discourse Analysis*. Vol. 4 (London: Academic Press, 1985), 2.

[31] Teun A. Van Dijk, *Handbook of Discourse Analysis*. Vol. 4, 18.

[32] Teun A. Van Dijk, *Handbook of Discourse Analysis*. Vol. 4, 19.

along Us versus Them dimensions, in which speakers of one group will generally tend to present themselves or their own group in positive terms, and other groups in negative terms."[33] His point is that one who desires to make transparent such an ideological dichotomy in discourse needs to analyze discourse in the following ways:

a. The context of the discourse is to be investigated in terms of historical, political or social background of a conflict and its main participants.
b. Groups, power relations and conflicts involved are to be analysed with deep insights
c. Positive and negative opinions about Us versus Them could be identified.
d. The presupposed and the implied should be made explicit
e. All formal structures, inclusive of lexical choice and syntactic structure, which in a way that help to (de) emphasize polarized group opinions are to critically viewed.[34]

1.4.3. Ruth Wodak

A wing of CDA, Discourse Sociolinguistics, related to Wodak and her colleagues in the Vienna School of Discourse Analysis. Wodak bases her model "on sociolinguistics in the Bernsteinian tradition and on the ideas of the Frankfurt school, especially those of Jürgen Habermas."[35] Wodak critiques on Discourse Sociolinguistics as: it is branch of the discipline called sociolinguistics which not only is explicitly dedicated to the study of the text in context, but also accords both factors equal importance. It is capable of identifying and describing the underlying mechanisms that take part in the disorders in discourse which are embedded in a particular context - whether they be in the structure and function

[33] Teun A. Van Dijk, *Handbook of Discourse Analysis*. Vol. 4. 22.

[34] Teun A. Van Dijk, *Handbook of Discourse Analysis*. Vol. 4, 1648.

[35] Ruth Wodak, *Disorders of Discourse* (London: Longman, 1995), 209.

of the media, or in institutions such as a hospital or a school-and have an indispensable impact on communication.

Wodak equips the theory with a lot of research in various institutional settings such as courts, schools, and hospitals, and on a variety of social issues such as sexism, racism and anti-Semitism. The discourse historical method has been a flagship work by work which was built up on the premises of the discourse of anti-Semitism that grasped her concentration in 1990. The term historical occupies a unique place in this approach. It denotes an attempt on the part of this approach "to integrate systematically all available background information in the analysis and interpretation of the many layers of a written or spoken text."[36] The results of Wodak and her colleagues' study showed that the context of the discourse had a significant impact on the structure, function, and context of the anti-Semitic utterances."[37]

In the discourse historical method approach it is believed that language "manifests social processes and interaction" and "constitutes" those processes as well.[38] In Wodak and Ludwig's view, discussing language this way demands three things in the minimal way: One, discourse "always involves power and ideologies. No interaction exists where power relations do not prevail and where values and norms do not have a relevant role."[39] Second, "discourse … is always historical, that is, it is connected synchronically and diachronically with other communicative events which are happening at the same time or which have happened before."[40] This is similar to Fairclough's notion of intertextuality, which aspect will be discussed in the next part. The third feature of Wodak's approach is that of interpretation. According to Wodak and Ludwig, readers and listeners, depending on their background knowledge and information and

[36] Ruth Wodak, *Disorders of Discourse,* 209.

[37] Ruth Wodak, *Disorders of Discourse*, 209.

[38] Ruth Wodak, C. Ludwig, *Challenges in a Changing World* (Vienna: Passagen Verlag,1999), 12.

[39] Ruth Wodak, C. Ludwig, *Challenges in a Changing World*, 12.

[40] Ruth Wodak, C. Ludwig, *Challenges in a Changing World*, 12.

their position, might have different interpretations of the same communicative event.[41] Therefore, Wodak & Ludwig assert that "the right interpretation does not exist; a hermeneutic approach is necessary. Interpretations can be more or less plausible or adequate, but they cannot be true."[42]

1.4.4. Fairclough

Fairclough's influential main theory pertaining to CDA is in vogue since the last decade. Even in his earlier work he gives the nomenclature Critical Language Study to his systematic study on language and discourse.[43] The objective of the theory is said to have, in Fairclough's words, "a contribution to the general rising of consciousness of exploitative social relations, through focusing upon language."[44] This aim in particular remains in his later work that further develops his approach so that it is now one of the most comprehensive frameworks of CDA a general overview of Fairclough's work in CDA, and a more detailed account of his framework for analyzing media discourse is presented in this section, as this acts as the foundation for the framework used in this study.

Chuliaraki and Fairclough had a strong contention that CDA "brings social science and linguistics ... together within a single theoretical and analytical framework, setting up a dialogue between them."[45] Like many of his fellow practitioners of CDA, the foundation for Fairclough's analytical framework has been SFL (Systematic Functional Linguistics). Fairclough's approach is also based upon many critical social theories such as Foucault's concept of orders of discourse, Gramsci's concept of

---

[41] Ruth Wodak, C. Ludwig, *Challenges in a Changing World*, 13.

[42] Ruth Wodak, C. Ludwig, *Challenges in a Changing World*, 13.

[43] Norman, Fairclough, *Critical Discourse Analysis*, 5.

[44] Norman, Fairclough, *Critical Discourse Analysis*, 4.

[45] Chouliaraki, Lilie and Norman Fairclough. *Discourse in Late Modernity – Rethinking Critical Discourse Analysis*, 6.

hegemony, Habermas' concept of colonization of discourses.[46] These expositions tired to identify the colonization in terms of knowledge. The Systemic models of education and the production of knowledge through translations also played an important role in the process of this colonization. All these models establish power and hierarchy as a product of these processes.

Chuliaraki and Fairclough had a firm belief in the contributory nature of the theory of CDA. They argue that, "the past two decades or so have been a period of profound economic social transformation on a global scale."[47] It is their belief that in spite of the fact that the changes are caused by people, the changes are perceived as 'part of nature' that is, changes and transformations have been the result of people's causal actions. The recent economic and social changes, according to Chuliaraki and Fairclough "are to a significant degree . . . transformations in the language, and discourse."[48] Thus, CDA can help by theorizing transformations and creating an awareness "of what is, how it has come to be, and what it might become, on the basis of which people may be able to make and remake their lives". Chuliaraki and Fairclough claim further that CDA of a communicative interaction sets out to show that the semiotic and linguistic features of the interaction are systematically connected with what is going on socially, and what is going on socially is indeed going on partly or wholly semiotically or linguistically.[49] CDA traces in an organized way the relations of conversion between the symbolic and non-symbolic discourse that is discursive and non-discursive.

Fairclough conforms to the idea that, linguistic analysis is concerned with presences as well as absences in texts that

---

[46] Chouliaraki, Lilie and Norman Fairclough. *Discourse in Late Modernity – Rethinking Critical Discourse Analysis*, 73.

[47] Chouliaraki, Lilie and Norman Fairclough. *Discourse in Late Modernity–Rethinking Critical Discourse Analysis*, 30.

[48] Chouliaraki, Lilie and Norman Fairclough. *Discourse in Late Modernity–Rethinking Critical Discourse Analysis*, 4.

[49] Chouliaraki, Lilie and Norman Fairclough. *Discourse in Late Modernity–Rethinking Critical Discourse Analysis*, 113.

could include "representations, categories of participant, and constructions of participant identity or participant relations". For Fairclough "Discourse practice straddles the division between society and culture on the one hand, and discourse, language and text on the other."[50]

1.5. Principles of CDA

In the backdrops of above discussions one can identify the following as the key principles of CDA.

1. Language is one among the social practices that represent the world.
2. Discourse/language use per se a form of social practice, acts as a representation and signification of other social practices and also it constitutes within itself other social practices like the exercise of power, domination, prejudice, resistance and so forth.
3. The meaning of the texts are constructed and acquired by the dialectical relationship between texts and the social subjects: writers and the readers, who are engaged with various degrees of choice as they get access to texts with multiple options of means of interpretation.
4. Linguistic features and structures cannot be classified as arbitrary in nature. They have a marked purpose whether or not the choices are conscious or unconscious.
5. Discourses are one of the causative factors to produce, exercise and reproduce power relations.
6. All speakers and writers operate from specific discursive practices originating in special interests and aims which involve inclusions and exclusions.
7. Discourse is historical that texts acquire their meanings within specific social, cultural and ideological contexts, and time and space.

---

[50] Chouliaraki, Lilie and Norman Fairclough. *Discourse in Late Modernity–Rethinking Critical Discourse Analysis*, 58.

8. Besides being preoccupied with interpreting texts, it also engages itself with explaining the texts.

1.6. Conclusion

Over the years, critical discourse analysis modified its methodological frame and become an interdisciplinary method. Therefore, critical Discourse Analysis is a very significant tool in order to identify the social and cultural systems of the society and narrations about the society through language. Biblical hermeneutics also identified the value and help of this methodology and have been a part of biblical scholarship. This study also considers CDS as an essential methodology to read the healing discourses in the Gospel of Mark.

Chapter 2

Gospel of Mark
Context and Content

2.1. Introduction

The Gospel of mark is considered as the first gospel ever written. Before Mark there were stories and clusters of stories about Jesus and some of them were written but none of those writings survived.[51] Norman R. Peterson observed that the Gospel according to Mark is a story world artistically constructed by immensely creative and powerful story teller.[52] But, content and meaning mark's gospel is considered as a historical gospel. The author of the Mark is writing history and not myth it means the

[51] Eugene Laverdiere, *The Beginning of the Gospel: Introducing the Gospel According to Mark* (Minnesota: The Liturgical Press, 1991), 1.

[52] Norman R. Peterson, "Point of View' in Mark's Narrative", in *Semeia* 12 (1978): 97-121.

author writes about a real human being, Jesus of Nazareth.[53] The Gospel of Mark uses different sources and parameters to develop its narratives. All these resources have been a key element in order to form the content of the Gospel of Mark. It is important to know the world that shaped the Gospel of mark; especially its content and theology. This chapter is an attempt to draw some basic geopolical concerns of the time which the gospel addressed.

2.2. Mark and Genre

The word "genre" means a literary kind or type. It refers to a sort of compact between an author and his reader in which the author tried to use various literary signals, will indicate to the reader what sort of document is being read and how it should be used. The genre signals in the text will help the reader and felicitate as a guide to the interpretation of the text.[54] When it comes to the discussion of Mark, from time to time it has been suggested that mark's Gospel is an example of Greek drama. There is certain plausibility to this suggestion but what sort of drama would mark gospel is the question. The studies state that it is certainly not a Greek comedy. Nor does it have the ending of a Greek tragedy. Therefore, while we consider that mark's is a dramatic gospel it does not seem to be a Greek tragedy. In contrary, it is a book of good news rather than tragedy.[55] Thus, the modern scholarship tried to identify the genre of mark Gospel in two wider frames of ancient literature, the historical monograph and the ancient biography.[56] An ancient biography certainly would include information about other persons

---

[53] Douglas R. Hare, *Mark* (Louisville: Westminster John Knox Press, 1996), 1.

[54] Ben Witherington III, *The Gospel of Mark: A Socio-Rhetorical Commentary* (Grand Rapids: William B. Eerdmans Publishing Company, 2001), 2.

[55] Ben Witherington III, *The Gospel of Mark: A Socio-Rhetorical Commentary,* 3.

[56] When it called as monographs it should not be considered or compared to the modern biographies which analyse the single character in detail rather it should consider as the biography of a time or period in which many figures and historical situations may appear and dissolve. Mark is very distinctive in this

and groups of people, but the major focus throughout the work would be on the central character. What is related to that person's character and personality would be included, what considered not related would be left out. Therefore, the genre itself is an exclusive model in which the central character in focus and what come in the backdrops are merely supportive characters or events for the central Figure of the Gospel Jesus.

2.3. Marken Context and Concerns

The reporting of the marken social context is connected with the context of the Galilee and Judea in the 20s and 30s.[57] The situations of the time set a volatile social space for the Jesus movements to act and involved. One of the core concerns of the movement is to radically reform early Judaism. Mark's gospel is remarkable because it is written about mostly ordinary people who were not by and large part of the social elite. Therefore it is reasonable to suppose that there were at least some of higher social level in mark audience. The Gospel of Mark tried to provide space to expose these conflicts between the communities and individuals belonging to various socio-political and religio-cultural categories of that time. One hand the gospel discussed about the roman colonial issues with the native community in Galilee and the other hand it also tried to portray the identity issue of the people related to cultural, social and religious context. Identifying these two aspects in the Gospel of mark is very important in order to understand the geopolitics of the Gospel of mark.

One can identify multiple faces of marken gospel in which it engaged with the concerns of the time. The Gospel of mark is distinctive in its reflections which originated from social, economic, political, cultural, and religious realities of its agrarian

---

order of frames from other Gospels. Other Gospels more or less tried to follow certain historical continuity but mark was absolutely away from this continuity.

[57] Ben Witherington III, *The Gospel of Mark: A Socio-Rhetoric Commentary*, 31.

context in the first century Roman occupied Palestine and Syria.[58] In subject matters the Gospel of Mark is an ideological one. The Gospel tried to put forth an ideology which emerged from the context of the land and the people of the land. The Gospel tried to present Jesus as the propagator of this ideology and the interactions and discourses Jesus engaged are the true expositions of this ideology. Therefore Mark's Gospel is not simply a witness to a prevailing view of the Christian faith or a confessional system of truth whose meaning can be determined by pinpointing its life situation. It is not the reproduction of any given reality. It is the reformulation of the already formulated Good news of Jesus Christ.[59] In order to identify the meaning and content of this reproduction and ideology one need to look in to the world that shaped the marken narration. For this the land, society, religion and the culture of the Marken community is inevitable. The following are some of the significant themes which shaped the discourses of the Gospel of Mark.

2.4. Mark and Galilee

In his exposition Luke Timothy Johnson argued that mark's specific emphasis on Galilee was a theological symbol as the world of the New Testament was shaped by roman colonialism.[60] The Galilee was a space witnessed many interactions between Christianity and the Roman Empire which also leads many religious and political conflicts. The inhabitants of Galilee were consider as people of low status – financial as well as social-and this lower status and its issues is one of the significant backdrops of Gospel of mark. This lower status of the people may identify in two ways. Firstly, the struggle against social oppression was accepted as an ideological strategy by the movement of Jesus in

---

[58] Herman C. Waetjen. *A Reordering of Power: A Socio-Political Reading of Mark's Gospel* (Minneapolis: Fortress Press, 1975), 1.

[59] Herman C. Waetjen. *A Reordering of Power: A Socio-Political Reading of Mark's Gospel,* 2.

[60] C.I. David Joy, *Mark and its Subalterns: A Hermeneutical Paradigm for a Post Colonial Context* (London: Equinox, 2008), 64.

Galilee. Secondly, this region witnessed multiple invasions by various groups and infiltration and migration.[61] Galilee was a place of cultural and economic interaction due to the presence of many ethnic and linguistic groups in Galilee. The Galilee was rejected and despised by the Judean Jews because of the radical mixture of the area and its distance from the temple in Jerusalem.[62] Therefore, the geo political situations of Galilee need to be addressed with special focus.

2.5. Jesus and Galilee

Jesus interaction and presence in the Galilee is one of the significant narrations of Gospel of Mark. The four canonical Gospels are unanimous in the depiction of Jesus as a travelling preacher and wonder-worker who visited numerous Galilean communities.[63] Jesus is said to have passed through Upper Galilee but the Gospel suggest he spent most of his time in Lower Galilee.[64] They identify only a few specific places by name. Jesus is frequently associated with Nazareth,[65] and Luke explicitly situates his synagogue sermon there.[66] John identifies cana as the site of two of Jesus' signs, and Luke describes Jesus' resurrection of a widow's son in Nain, a short distance to the south of Galilee in the Jezreel.[67] Most of the Galilean communities mentioned by name are near the sea

---

[61] C.I. David Joy, *Mark and its Subalterns: A Hermeneutical Paradigm for a Post Colonial Context,* 64.

[62] C.I. David Joy, *Mark and its Subalterns: A Hermeneutical Paradigm for a Post Colonial Context,* 64.

[63] The episodes of these visits may find out from Mark 1:39, Matthew 4.23, Mark 6:6, Matthew 9:35, Luke 8:1.

[64] See Mark 7:24-30; Matthew 15:21-28; Mark 8:27-33; Matthew 16: 13-23.

[65] See Mark 1:9,24; 10:47, 14:67, 16:6. Matthew 21:11, 26:71; Luke 18:37, 24:19; John 1:45-46, 18:5-7, 19:19.

[66] See Luke 4:16-30; Mark 6:1 and Mathew 13:54.

[67] See John 2:1-11, 4:46-54; Luke 7:11-17.

of Galilee: Capernaum,[68] Bethsaida;[69] Chorazin;[70] Gennesaret;[71] and Magdala.[72] These traditions tried to portray that the Sea of Galilee region was the primary area of Jesus' activity.

The gospel narrations supports in different levels that gentile mission was the primary goal of Jesus movement.[73] It got an important part of Jesus' ministry. Galilee also played an important role in the development of Jesus' identity. It is clear that the early Christian claims about messianic status of Jesus were highly contentious, and the Gospel accounts also portrayed this issue in many ways. Theses controversies also played an important role in the making of Christology in Galilean context. Therefore, Galilean context also given rise to images of messiah those were different from those which were formulated among the Jewish religious elites.[74]

Jesus would have met gentiles during his ministry, especially in the area around the Sea of Galilee. But, locating the frequency or the count of such interaction is impossible within the limited sources. But, from the limited sources one thing is clear that the geographical focus of Jesus' ministry was Galilee.[75]

2.6. Mark and the Geo Political Structure of Galilee

Geographically this northernmost district of Palestine was a little island in the midst of unfriendly seas.[76] On all sides were Gentile

[68] See Mark 1:21, 2:1-12, 9:33; Matthew 4:13, 8:5-13, 17:24-27, 9:1-8; Luke 4:23, 4:31, 7:1-10; John 2:12, 6:24, 6:59.

[69] Mark 8:22; Matthew 11:20-24; Luke 9:10, 10:13-15.

[70] Matthew 11:20-24, Luke 10:13-15.

[71] Mark 6:53, Matthew 14:34.

[72] Matthew 15:39.

[73] Mark A. Chancey. *The Myth of a Gentile Galilee* (New York: Cambridge University Press, 2002), 174.

[74] Sean Freyne. *Galilee and Gospel* (Boston: Brill Academic Publishers, Inc, 2002), 261.

[75] Mark A. Chancey. *The Myth of a Gentile Galilee,* 175.

[76] K.W. Clark, "Galilee," in *The Interpreter's Dictionary of the Bible, Vol. 2.* ed. George A. Buttrick (New York: Abingdon Press, 1972), 347.

nations separating it from Judea to the south. It early acquired the name in the Old Testament of "Galilee of the Gentiles" or "Galilee of the nations" (Isaiah 9:1). For the Jews living in Galilee, their home was not only surrounded, but also inhabited by Phoenicians, Syrians, Arabs, Greeks, Romans and others. It was a multicultural, multiracial region, biologically and culturally mixed. Thus the name "Galilee of the nations," or "of the Gentiles," reflected a reputation for racial variety and mixture.[77] It was indeed a mixture of "all nations" community, and the Galileans were racially and culturally mixed. The geography of Galilee becomes relevant in this study as there is a relationship between geography and human life.[78] The Jesus movements and its events had been conditioned by the religious and cultural forces in Galilean life. Galilee was far from Jerusalem, which means far from the center of theology and religion; Galilee was far from Rome, which means it was far from the center of law and government; Galilee was far from Athens, which means it was far from the center of culture and the arts.[79] As far as the southern Jews were concerned, nothing good could ever come out of Galilee, except a bunch of rabble rousers, half-breeds, ruthless, unrighteous people who despise the teachings of God. Thus Galileans were regarded as fools, heretics and rebels.

Galilee also was a rich farming region, so rich in soil and pasturage, that Josephus, the first century Jewish historian, once described Galilee as a place where "even the most indolent are tempted by these facilities to devote themselves to agriculture."[80] The terms 'peasants,' 'the common people,' the 'am ha-arez' (the people of the land) were all terms applied to Galileans, all of which carried the stigma of a religiously uneducated people. The existence of large estates and fertile lands created an atmosphere

---

[77] K. W. Clark, "Galilee," in *The Interpreter's Dictionary of the Bible, Vol. 2.* ed. George A. Buttrick, 345.

[78] C.I. David Joy, *Mark and its Subalterns: A Hermeneutical Paradigm for a Post Colonial Context,* 65.

[79] K. W. Clark. "Galilee," in *The Interpreter's Dictionary of the Bible, Vol. 2.* ed. George A. Buttrick, 345.

[80] Vermes, Geza. *Jesus the Jew* (London: William Collins Sons, 1977), 46.

of feudalism which resulted in deep exploitation of labour and dignity of the people. The possibility of a socio-political situation with marginalisation in terms of land and power may be recognized from this context. The accumulation of wealth and land by certain communities or people will naturally open up the situation of social order and discrimination. Therefore there should be natural resistance, where there is a power there is a resistance, the resistance against the oppressive structure of the system. As a result of this resistance the Galileans were marked as the revolutionaries, because this resistance was part of their life.[81]

We cannot fully identify the feelings of Judean Jews towards Galileans, unless we understand Jewish insistence on ancestral and racial purity. The Jews held that only Israelites of pure ancestry made up the pure Israel.[82] Thus, "even the simple Israelite knew his immediate ancestors and could point to which of the twelve tribes he belonged."[83] After the exile, genealogies became important in order to separate pure families from those racially mixed, as a result of the racial-mixing practices of the Assyrians. The books of Ezra, Nehemiah and 1 and 2 Chronicles, written after the exile, are all filled with genealogical lists portrayed the intention of the post exile communities. In the post-exilic period, these lists were important in order to determine who was a pure Israelite. A person should prove their ancestral purity to at least five generations to be a priest nor could they hold a public office without pure ancestry. Proof of pure ancestry was important for a woman to marry into a priestly family.[84] A person's salvation also depended on their ancestral purity. And so Galileans, by their racial and cultural mixture were deprived of earthly social positions and heavenly inheritance as they were predestined to

---

[81] C.I. David Joy, *Mark and its Subalterns: A Hermeneutical Paradigm for a Post Colonial Context,* 65.

[82] Joachim Jeremias, *Jerusalem In the Time of Jesus* (Philadelphia: Fortress Press, 1969), 275-302.

[83] Joachim Jeremias, *Jerusalem In the Time of Jesus,* 275.

[84] Joachim Jeremias, *Jerusalem In the Time of Jesus,* 275.

hell. This salvation discourses are very evident in the healing stories of the Mark Gospel.

2.6.1. Hellenism, Greco-Roman Culture, and Paganism

The shape and functioning of the Ancient Galilee in its cultural aspects need much attention. Any discussion on the cultural atmosphere of the Ancient Galilee must keep in mind that the local culture is predominantly that of Jews.[85] The ancient Galilee was deeply affected by Greco-Roman culture as well. Hellenism denotes the presence of Greek culture and Greco-roman culture denotes the added influence of Roman culture.[86] Paganism denotes the worship of any diet other than the Jewish and Christian God. In the Galilean context many of the Hellenistic or Greco-Roman Culture has been misinterpreted as evidence for paganism. Therefore, the presence of Hellenism in a particular place does not necessarily indicate the presence of pagans and also the presence of pagans does not necessarily imply the presence of Hellenism. Martin Hengel in his thesis observed that a community with widespread use of Greek language, the presence of Greek architectural forms and ideologies and thoughts without having a large number of gentiles are Jewish.[87]

2.7. Forms of Religious Expressions

There are various clusters of first-century religious expression which can be identified in the Gospel of mark. In the healing stories there will be always confrontations between Jesus and the religious authorities of the time. The following are some of the important Jewish religious forms prevailed in the marken narratives.

[85] Mark A. Chancey. *The Myth of a Gentile Galilee,* 179.

[86] Mark A. Chancey. *The Myth of a Gentile Galilee,* 7.

[87] Martin Hengel. *The "Hellenizatio" of Judaea in the first century after Christ* (London: SCM Press, 1989), 32.

2.7.1. The Pharisees

Pharisees, the religious domain, most frequently mentioned in the New Testament, are pointed out as 'the most acute interpreters of law.'[88] The Gospels and Paul has different view on Pharisees and their involvements in the early church as well as the Jesus' time. Paul many a time tried to propose a positive idea. But, the Gospel tried to portray them as a negative character, also positive allusions occur. In Luke 13:31, for instance, the Pharisees seek to warn Jesus of Herod's plan for kill him. But, Gospel of Matthew tried to maligns the Pharisees in harshly negative terms like Vipers,[89] hypocrites,[90] blind guides,[91] murderers of the prophets,[92] and white washed tombs.[93] In the custom of the Pharisees the observance of law and purity is very strong. They used to take ritual bath after returning from the market place, after touching a copse, or after having certain bodily discharge in order to use clean hands in prayer before their meals. They ritualistically cleansed, not merely washed vessels, cup etc.[94] Pharisees excluded unclean persons such as tax collectors, the ill, the physically handicapped, or the emotionally disturbed from table fellowship.[95] The Gospel tried to set Pharisees as the life of rituals. In priestly religion, priests declared what was clean and unclean and what is acceptable before God and not. In order to establish the purity rules they used to draw boundaries not only between Jews and gentiles, but also between Jews and Jews. Degree of purity determines the degree of access to God.[96] Thus, by declaring what was clean and

---

[88] Calvin J. Roetzel, *The World that Shaped the New Testament* (Atlanta: John Knox Press, 1973), 25.

[89] See Matthew 3:7; 12:34; 23:33.

[90] See Matthew 23:23, 27.

[91] See Matthew 23:16, 24.

[92] See Matthew 23:31.

[93] See Matthew 23:27.

[94] See Mark 7:3-4.

[95] See Mark 2:16.

[96] Frederick J. Murphy. *The Religious World of Jesus* (Nashville: Abingdon Press, 1991), 238.

unclean the priests were potentially in control of society. In the Gospel of Mark Jesus tries to problamatize and challenged this authority and discriminations in the healing stories. Pharisiaism in Jesus' period was quietistic and apolitical, concerned primarily with matters of ritual.[97] In Rivkin's view the writing of Josephus, rabbinic traditions, the Apocrypha and Pseudepigrapha of the Old Testament and the New Testament all share a common view that the Pharisees were popular with the masses, served as a scholar class interpreting both oral and written traditions, believed in individual immorality, and promulgated new law.

2.7.2. The Sadducees

The Pharisees are the dominated group in the New Testament, while the Sadducees recede into the background.[98] The Sadducees may describe as a small group segment of the ruling class. But, it is sure that not all members of the ruling class were Sadducees. The Sadducees existed at least from the second half of the second century BCE to the destruction of Jerusalem in 70 CE. In rabbinic literature Sadducees are portrayed as the community who follows ritual purity and Sabbath observance. They were members of the ruling class, and they did not believe in resurrection.[99] Josephus and New testament agrees on this point. In Act 4:1 and 5:17, the Sadducees are associated with the chief priests and the captain of the temple. This agree that the Josephus' claim that they supported by the ruling class.[100] Mark mentioned the Sadducees only one time regarding the question of resurrection.[101] Their denial of the resurrection shows that they "know neither the scripture nor the

---

[97] Ellis Rivkin, *A Hidden Revolution: The Pharisees' Search for the Kingdom within* (Nashville: Abingdon, 1978), 72-75.

[98] Gunter Stemberger, *Jewish Contemporaries of Jesus: Pharisees, Sadducees, Essenes* (Minneapolis: Fortress Press, 1995), 21.

[99] Frederick J. Murphy. *The Religious World of Jesus* (Nashville: Abingdon press, 1991), 239.

[100] Frederick J. Murphy. *The Religious World of Jesus,* 242.

[101] See Mark 12:18-27.

power of God."[102] They are confused because of their knowledge and agonies of their philosophies. These thoughts and encounters had been one of the significant contexts which shaped the conceptual frames of Gospel of Mark.

2.8. Conclusion

The content of the Gospel of Mark cannot be traced out or read out without the context that shaped the marken narratives. This includes communities, ideologies, philosophies, religious thoughts, social orders, issues of class, gender and identities etc. This chapter tried to outline some of the important elements which were very fundamental in the geopolitical context of the marken community and time. These understanding will make significant inputs in order to identify the discourses of Jesus with the communities in the Gospel of mark. The healing discourse in the Gospel of Mark also needs to address on the backdrops of these wider understandings of geopolitics of the land.

---

[102] See Mark 12:24.

Chapter 3

Healing Stories as Social Discourse

3.1. Introduction

Healing stories are one of the predominant literary units of the New Testament narratives especially the Gospel narratives. Over one fifth of the literary units of the synoptic gospels contain either descriptions or allusions to the healings and exorcism of Jesus and his disciples.[103] Unfathomable healing wonders and uncountable miracles of Jesus, that were performed 'out of difficulties' have caught the fascination of theorists, theologians and common people at any given time alike. Since the stories provide believers across societies with strong fodder to affirming of faith, and these sections offer the high possibility to discern the divine Jesus and historical Jesus, studying them as Social Discourses becomes an inevitable process. The healing stories offer space to talk about the marginalised identities of the people through a web of signifiers

[103] Howard Clark Kee, *Medicine, Miracle and Magic in New Testament Times* (Cambridge: Cambridge University Press, 1986), 1.

– social, gender, religious, ethnic and racial. They contain social as well as religious task. Every healing story is an attempt to reimagining the socio-religious-political and cultural context of the land and its people. This aspect of healing stories needs wider attention in order to map them as a socio-political discourse in the Jesus' movement.

Graham Stanton takes into consideration the framework of seventeen narratives of healings in the gospels including three vivification stories. According to Stanton's argument, it cannot be claimed that Jesus' miraculous power flourished due to the vulnerable and naive nature of the ancient world; he points out at the proof of existent tendency in Jewish antiquity of narrating the miracles with outspoken scepticism and trying to reason out with other possible explanations for those actions.[104] Still Stanton is not able to grasp the genuine reason that propelled Jesus' miracles. The factors like the faith of the individual, the compassion of Jesus, and the attraction of the crowd to Jesus are randomly zoomed into the circle of wide motives, but Stanton's firm opinion is that they could not be the foundational motives for His miracles. He posits that investing close attention to the individuals and circumstances involved in the healing stories can help throw light onto the professed intention of Jesus. According to Stanton:

> Jesus healed people with many kinds of disability. The lepers healed by Jesus may have had some kind of skin disease, i.e., not what we known as Hansen's disease; but in the eyes of many, touching a leper was a violation of ritual regulations (Mark 1. 40-45; Luke 17:11-19; Lev 13:45-60). As Kee (1986:78-79) has emphasised, Jesus healed persons who were considered by some of his contemporaries to be 'off-limits' by the standards of Jewish piety, by reason of their race (Mark 7:24-30), their place of residence

[104] Graham Stanton, "Message and Miracles", in *The Cambridge Companion of Jesus* ed. Markus Bockmuchl (Cambridge: Cambridge University Press, 2001), 66.

> (Mark 5:1-20) in a tomb in pagan territory, or their ritual impurity (5:25-34, a women with menstrual flow). Although a full discussion is not possible here, many of the healing and exorcism of Jesus were an indication of his full acceptance of those who were socially and religiously marginalized.[105]

The healing stories offer space to talk about the marginalised identities of the people through a web of signifiers – social, gender, religious, ethnic and racial. Thus, healing stories contains a social as well as a religious task. Every healing story is an attempt to reimaging the socio-religious-political and cultural context of the land and its people. This aspect of healing stories needs wider attention in order to map the healing stories as a socio-political discourse in the Jesus movement.

3.2. Miracle in the Greco-Roman World

According to the Gospel narratives one can identify Jesus' immediate milieu was Israelite, therefore the miracle stories always have concentrated on the understanding of miracle in a Jewish context.[106] But, first century Palestine was known for the Greco-Roman invasion and influences. Classical form critics such as Rudolph Bultmann and Martin Dibelius suggested that most of the miracle stories in the Gospel were formed on Hellenistic models for the purpose of missionary propaganda. Along with Rudolph Bultmann and Martin Dibelius several other scholars also have pointed that the Gospel Miracle stories are designed to portray Jesus as a '*theios aner*' (Divine Man) for the benefit of a Greco-Roman audience who would recognize the type and be suitably impressed by it.[107] In the healing stories also one can identify this portrayal of Jesus; the discourse model of the healing

---

[105] Graham Stanton, "Message and Miracles", in *The Cambridge Companion of Jesus* ed. Markus Bockmuehl, 68.

[106] Eric Eve. *The Healer from Nazareth: Jesus Miracles in Historical Context* (London: SPCK, 2009), 39.

[107] Eric Eve. *The Healer from Nazareth: Jesus Miracles in Historical Context,* 40.

stories itself played an important role in making this divine identity and attributing it to Jesus. This obviously unveils Jesus' identity as a hierarchical one with power and holiness. Therefore, one of the fundamental tasks of the healing stories are to develop a hierarchical space for Jesus in order to establish His movement and qualify its genuineness before the socio-religious context of Greco-Roman World. It has also been argued that the category of *theios aner* is not necessary to account for the miracle stories in Mark, which can be perfectly well accounted from a Jewish background.[108]

There is a conceptual error in bracketing whole Greco-Roman antiquity together as its attitudes to miracles were uniform across classes, culture and centuries. There are many evidences suggesting that among the educated upper classes, scepticism towards the miracle procedures reached a peak in the first century BCE.[109] Therefore, it is a mistake to take miracle stories from the pagan religious propaganda of the second and third centuries CE as automatically indicative of their use in the first.[110]

The main thing to note about the healing miracles in the Greco-Roman world is that the healing shrines were a recognized institution of antiquity, a place where society could conveniently place the sick related issues to be taken care of. This emphasizes that the god performing the miracle was not a visible presence like Jesus or one of the Israelite prophets. It is also noted that a very different social role is played by an institutional healing shrine from that played by a charismatic healer like Jesus. Therefore, Jesus' personal presence in the healing stories of the Gospel and his personal involvement in the process of healing is one of the

---

[108] Eric Eve. *The Healer from Nazareth: Jesus Miracles in Historical Context,* 40.

[109] Robert M. Grant, *Miracle and Natural Law in Greco-Roman and Early Christian Thought* (Amsterdam: Noord-hollandsche Uitgevers – Maatschapij, 1952), 4.

[110] Howard C. Kee, *Medicine, Miracle and Magic in New Testament Times,* 272.

significant religious and cultural acts in which he proposed an alternative for being healed.

Many of the healing miracle stories in Greco–Roman antiquity come, not from accounts of charismatic miracle-working figure like Jesus of Nazareth, but from inscription at healing shrines such as Epidauros[9]. There are number of gods including Isis and sarapis who are associated with healing but the chief healing God of Greco-Roman antiquity was Asclepius. Asclepius was not an earthly human physician but he was considered as god, since he had a miraculous healing cult associated with him. All these historical mentioning raise one fact in general that the Greco-Roman context was rich in the healing and miraculous content. When Jesus came into the picture it was neither a maiden nor an old act rather it simply resonated the continuity of the miracle discourses in the Greco-Roman world. Therefore, the land and its people tried to place Jesus' act also on the frame and content of the existing healing discourses and stories. But, Jesus actually tried to adopt the frame of miracle stories to develop an alternative movement. This is very important when it comes to the study of the healing stories and its discourse analysis.

3.3. Healing Stories and Gospel

According to the Gospel narratives Jesus got the identity as a miracle worker in the very beginning of his public ministry. This reputation grew and spread wherever he went. Quite apart from his many acts of healing, he also did things which clash with normal natural laws, such as walking on water, calming a storm and using very little resources to feed large crowds. He raised dead people to life again and overcame a wide variety of evil forces. According to the four gospels, he continued to do such things throughout his ministry until finally he himself rose again from death after his public execution, and ascended into the clouds in front of a crowd to witness.

Mark's Gospel is very significant as far as the miracle stories are concerned. Its treatment of miracle is arguably both the most complete and complex of the four gospels. Mark has the highest concentration of miraculous material of any of the Gospels, particularly in the first half of the book.[111]Moreover, Mark's miracle stories are far from being a random selection of stunning deeds; they have been arranged with order and purpose. The problem is determining what precisely that order and purpose is.[112] This order is very important for the methodology of this thesis. The structure of Mark's narratives and stories clearly states one thing that Mark's gospel is both a story about Jesus and an address to Christians of Mark's own day. There is also often both surface and a symbolic meaning, particularly in some of the miracle stories. Allan Richardson observes that the miracle stories in the Mark gospel are the products of profound meditation upon the significance of the person and actions of Jesus, and their interest centres in their theological rather than in their historical character. He also observes that the healing stories in Mark Gospel are part of the continuity of the healing story tradition of the land and Mark preserved that tradition in his Gospel as well.[113] Therefore, we cannot look upon Mark as in any sense as an innovator; he is rather the preserver and scribe of the tradition by which he himself has been instructed. The study of the Marken healing stories brings out one interesting fact that Mark is more interested in the theological implications of the matter than in the construction of a consistent historical narrative or of a neatly-finished literary biography.[114]

3.4. Healing Stories and Social Discourse

The social function of healing stories is important to notice. Traditions can be understood only in terms of the real context of social and historical life. Primitive Christian miracle stories are

---

[111] In the first half of the book one can identify 209 out of Mark's 666 verses are in some way connected with miracle.

[112] Graham H. Twelftree, *Jesus the Miracle Worker: A Historical and Theological Study* (Downers Grove, IL: InterVarsity Press, 1999), 57.

[113] Alan Richardson, *The Miracle Stories of The Gospel* (London: SCM, 1963), 101.

[114] Alan Richardson, *The Miracle Stories of The Gospel,* 103.

symbolic interactions on the part of groups, within ancient society. Their social dimensions can be explored in two directions. First, they reflect social factors which unconsciously influenced both story-tellers and audiences and, second, they project a particular form of social relationship.[115] Both aspects are very crucial in order to identify the purpose of healing discourse.

Primitive Christian miracle stories are rooted in the predominantly rural world of Galilee. E. Trocme has suggested that they are expressions of a quasi – animistic rural attitude from the border areas of Syria and Palestine and in contrast to the heavily ethically oriented sayings tradition, which comes from the urban world of Jerusalem.[116] Trocme tried to place the sociological point that there is a structural connection between belief in miracle and a rural environment. The whole of the synoptic tradition, including the sayings, is rural in character. The parables take us into the world of farmers and fisherman, vine-growers and shepherds. There is no basis for a general assumption that a rural population at this period would be more susceptible to belief in demon and forces than an urban one. The synoptic tradition does come from a predominantly rural area surrounded by two series of Hellenistic cities; the cities on the coast of the Mediterranean and those to the east of the Jordan, the so-called 'Decapolis', and it is quite possible that this background create some effect on the characters of the miracle stories.[117]

3.5. Power and Hierarchy in Healing Stories

The movement initiated by Jesus was certainly not an affair of the upper classes. In Galilee Jesus turned to the social and political outcasts. The people who followed Jesus were the 'crowd', the humble people. It is true that primitive Christianity soon had members from higher classes, but the miracle stories, in the simplicity of their theology, in the simplicity of their narrative, but

---

[115] Gerd Theissen, *The Miracle Stories of the Early Christian Tradition* (Edinburgh: T&T Clark, 1983), 231.

[116] Gerd Theissen, *The Miracle Stories of the Early Christian Tradition,* 246.

[117] Gerd Theissen, *The Miracle Stories of the Early Christian Tradition,* 247.

above all in their subject matter, turned out to be the alternate of power. According to Foucault power is not a 'thing, or a capacity' which can be owned either by State, social class or particular individual. Instead it is a relation among different individuals and groups and only exists when it is being exercised.[118] Therefore in terms of power, human relationships are important than institutions and governments. Moreover power reaches into the very grain of individuals, touches their bodies and inserts itself into their actions and attitudes, their discourses, learning processes and everyday lives.[119] In the context of healing stories one can identify the functioning of power and hierarchy. The end result of every healing discourse portrayed the authority and hierarchy of Jesus. Sometimes this hierarchy is over against the religious groups; sometimes this hierarchy is over against the state and power structures of the society. Therefore, healing stories functioned as a plot to develop the alternative power which comes through Jesus over against the existing socio-political-religious orders. Every existing order in knowledge, society, and culture is limited and that needs to be challenged time to time. Power relations are embedded in social life. Healing stories and the discourses opens this challenge. Genealogical analysis reveals the body as an object of knowledge and as a target for exercise of power. The body is shown to be located in a political field, invested with power relations that render it docile and productive, and thus politically and economically useful.[120] In the healing stories the healed body may consider as a plot to exercise this power and also to establish new order of power. Prior to healing the body was the located in a different social order and after healing the body has been moved to a different social order. Discourse is the fundamental factor which leads this transition. Therefore, the power and hierarchy should be identified as the important characteristics of the healing

[118] Clare O'Farrell, *Michel Foucault* (New Delhi: Sage Publication, 2005), 99.

[119] Michel Foucault, *Discipline and Punish* (New York: Vintage Book, 1979), 30.

[120] Barry Smart, *Michel Foucault*, (London: Routledge Press, 2002), 75.

discourse. Discourse Analysis tries to identify the play of power in the healing Discourse.

3.6. Healing Atories and its Significance

The significance attached to miracles at the time of Jesus was one of the important factors to be identified. According to the early historical document of Josephus, Pseudo-Philo and Philo of Alexandria we could get some insights regarding this concern. According to Josephus, miracles are the most striking examples of the workings of God's providence, which is understood as God's retributive Justice working itself out in history. For Pseudo-philo the function of miracle is often to punish the wicked, rescue the righteous, or protect the covenant people. For Philo of Alexandria, miracle is more important in defining God as the biblical God who acts, rather than the Aristotelian unmoved mover, stoic world-soul, or abstract Platonic idea. They may also offer a propagandist function, indirectly glorifying Judaism by showing what great things God did on its behalf. In all these expressions of the writers, miracles have evidential value, for Josephus it is to accredit God's agent; for pseudo-philo, they may be used by the faithful to discern God's will; for Philo of Alexandria, they demonstrate the reality of God's will and power.[121]

The healing stories have a social significance and it is well placed in the doctrinal formula 'your faith has saved you'. The miracle stories promise rescue, salvation, and redemption. The miracle stories also have a missionary intention.[122] This intention can be reconstructed from the analogy of miracles and miracle-workers. It is the task of the apostles to preach and heal.[123] Early Church father Origen repeatedly emphasises the missionary significance of miracles. This missionary intention of miracles makes it very clear that the miracle stories have a similar intention.

---

[121] Eric Eve. *The Healer from Nazareth: Jesus Miracles in Historical Context,* 47.

[122] Gerd Theissen. *The Miracle Stories of the Early Christian Tradition* (Edinburgh: T&T Clark, 1983), 264.

[123] See Luke 10:8; Matthew 10:7; Mark 3:15; 6:15.

The intention of the miracle stories is also intended to bear witness to a revelation of God which is directed to the whole world and seeks to bring all human beings to recognise that revelation.[124] Therefore, one can look at miracle stories as a collective symbolic action in which a new way of life is opened up; as this function transcends both the social conditions in which the ancient Christian belief in miracles was moulded and the intentions it attributes to itself.

3.7. Theology of Healing Stories

The synoptic healing stories can also be placed in a wider theological framework. Refuting any trace of either medical techniques or the rhetoric of diagnosis and prescription for diseases commonly found in the roman medical tradition of the first century, or anything that can be labelled as magic within the healing stories of Jesus, Howard Clark Kee understands the healing of Jesus in a proleptic sense in relation to the reign of God:

> The frame work of meaning in which these stories of Jesus' healing are told is not one which assumes that the proper formula or the correct technique will produce the desired results. Rather the healings and exorcism are placed in a larger structure which sees what is happening as clues are foretastes of a new situation in which the purpose of God will finally be accomplished in the creation and his people will be vindicated and at peace.[125]

Discounting the valence of the umbrella metaphor of 'Jesus the teacher' under which the quest for historical Jesus has been predominantly undertaken, Stevan L. Davies in his *Jesus the Healer (1995)* argues that such studies which have as their paradigmatic locus this single ruling metaphor have more often than not led to not only a problematic conceptual diversity, but also

---

[124] Gerd Theissen. *The Miracle Stories of the Early Christian Tradition,* 262.

[125] Howard C. Kee, *Medicine, Miracle and Magic in New Testament Times,* 79.

indicate and accentuate the flawed nature of scholarly attempts to produce a comprehensive and credible portrait of Jesus' teachings, a fact overtly attested by the plethora of mutually inconsistent modalities which have been proposed for understanding Jesus' teachings.[126]According to him the thesis Jesus as teacher is highly estranged in its conformity with evidence. Therefore, against this metaphor of Jesus the Teacher Davies proposes a paradigmatic shift to 'Jesus the Healer' which he feels is more relevant and appropriate:

The ruling metaphor, or paradigm, that does reveal an historical Jesus who did pretty much what the New Testament says he did, and who is *not* a social type never before or since heard of in the world (e.g., a peasant Jewish cynic) is the metaphor of Jesus the Healer. Start with the question "how did he heal" rather than the question "what did he teach" and many things become clear.[127]

However, Davies doesn't take the theological importance of healing stories with an appropriate consideration. Eric Lott tried to make a critical observation on Davis' thesis. Lott observes that the subjection of the healing stories to Davies' view, of Jesus as a spirit possessed ecstatic who like other shaman figures effected healing by being taken over by another persona and drew others into sharing his own 'dissociative religious trance', is unnecessarily limiting.[128] Lott makes clear that the virtual impossibility of arriving upon an authentic picture of Jesus or of his liberating work, unless his healing acts are crucial to this picture. Exclaiming his perplexity that 'healing' hasn't figured as an interpretative category, as a hermeneutical key, Lott says that a psyco-anthropological way of reading these stories could prove fruitful in trying to work out a more authentic life centred theologies.[129]

---

[126] Stevan L. Davies, *Jesus the Healer* (London: SCM Press, 1995), 14.

[127] Stevan L. Davies, *Jesus the Healer,* 15.

[128] Eric J. Lott, *Healing Wings: Acts of Jesus for Human Wholeness* (Bangalore: Asian Trading Corporation, 1998), 1.

[129] Eric J. Lott, *Healing Wings: Acts of Jesus for Human Wholeness,* 2.

3.8. Conclusion

Outside the New Testament there is little interest in healing miracles in Jewish texts, and Jesus is unique in the surviving Jewish literature of the time in having a whole series of healing and exorcism stories attributed to him. The largest number of Greco-roman healing stories are associated with shrines like the Asclepium at Epidauros rather that with charismatic miracle – workers. Jesus stands out as being exceptional in the miracle works whether against Israelite or Greco-roman models of healing. One can identify three important features of the healing stories particularly for interpreting the ministry of healing and exorcism. The healing stories functioned as a hope and metaphor for national restoration, the tradition of the eschatological Davidic shepherd who would heal and feed the flock, and the expectation of the final defeat of demonic powers.[130]

On the other hand healing stories in the Gospel has a specific social task. The healing discourse opens the social intentions of the healing stories of Jesus. Power, hierarchy, culture, religious and political models of dominance has been a matter of problematizing in the healing stories. This could be the analytical task of the next chapter through the methodological frame of Critical Discourse.

---

[130] Eric eve. *The Healer from Nazareth: Jesus Miracles in Historical Context* (London: SPCK, 2009), 50.

Chapter 4

Healing Stories in Mark 2:1-12, Mark 5:1-12, and Mark: 10:46-52 Critical Discourse Analysis

4.1. Introduction

This chapter tries to study the concern of the text using the methodology of Critical Discourse Analysis. Author, audience, and text in communicative events, are elements probed in seriously in Discourse Analysis and these paraphernalia are viewed as a network of influences contributing to the production and consumption of communicative events. Discourse analysts seek to interpret a speaker/author's role in the production of discourses.[131] The term "author" here is not a static one but takes into account such things as or iginal and implied authors (and readers). This does not alter the fact that much of discourse

[131] J. P. Louw, "Reading a Text as Discourse," in *Linguistics and New Testament Interpretation: Essays on Discourse Analysis* ed. D. A. Black (Nashville: Broadman, 1992), 20.

analysis has been concerned with naturally occurring texts and, consequently, how original speakers/authors create those texts and how original listeners/readers process them.

4.2. Mark 2:1-12: Text and Context

Though the analysis focused on Mark 2:1-12 discussion in regard to the context of the text demands the understanding of wider periscope i.e. Mark 2:1-3:6. Most of the exegetes consider Mark 2:1-3:6 entirely or partly a pre-Marcan collection or a part of a larger collection. One of the major evidences resulting in the studies to this assumption is the thematic and formal compactness of Mark 2:1-3:6. Some of the scholars give lot of importance to Mark 3:6 in establishing Mark 2:1-3:6 as a pre-Marcan tradition. All these assumptions might be considered as the result not so much of historical events but rather of a well–planned composition with a deliberation to present an explanation for the anti – Jesus attitude of the Jews and for Jesus' death.

The preceding and following sections of Mark 2:1-3:6, depict the crowds being presented as coming to Jesus, and in which there is no mention of conflict. It is a clearly distinguishing factor from Mark 2:1-3:6 which is a self contained and well – constructed unit set in frames and in stark contrast with the preceding and succeeding sections. All these indications point in the direction of a Marcan insertion of Mark 2:1-3:6 into a wider context.

The periscope begins with the mentioning of Jesus' entry to Capernaum. The preceding healing of the leper ends with the leper spreading the news and he could no longer openly enter any public space because of the huge crowd. But, Mark 2:1 has Jesus returning to Capernaum. According to Mark, the first thing Jesus does after becoming of not able to enter a city is to enter a city.

4.2.1. Analysis

The Analysis is focused on three different categories. The first category is the body and the social location of the body and this section tries to identify the importance of body in the healing discourse. Body is seen as a source of multiple contexts of the existing system of thought and also looks at the way the body has been problamatized in the healing Discourse. Secondly, analysis of the language in the healing discourses. This part of the analysis focuses on the language and linguistic aspects which played an important role in forming the healing discourse as Socio-Political Discourse of the time. This analysis also tries to locate the place of healing Discourses in the Jesus Movement beyond 'Miracle work.'[132] Thirdly, the analysis is related to the post healed body in order to identify the task of the discourse. This part of the analysis will bring forth the alternatives which Jesus proposed through the healing stories. The alternative carries the problematization of the existing order as well. The study also tries to explore in linguistic dimension for certain words.

4.2.2. Body and Social Location

4.2.2.1. Placing of Body

The methodology of the analysis considers body as a social variable in order to identify social construct through body. Hence, the placing of the body and the peoples and elements involved in the placing of the body become paramount. In the healing story of the paralysed, four men arrived bearing a paralyzed person on a mat, but they are unable to present him to Jesus for healing because the way is completely blocked. So they lift the paralyzed upon the roof of the house and lower the person directly in front of Jesus. These actions signify deliberate faith in Jesus and his healing power. And Jesus valued the faith of the people who carried the paralyzed and declared "your sins are forgiven". Till that moment, Jesus had uttered nothing about the forgiveness of sin to any of the diseased and demon possessed whom he had

---

[132] The study place the argument that the healing stories are not mere miracle works. The functioning and portrayal of the healing discourses marked the significant identity of the healing stories. It always carries the function of Socio-political Discourse and put forth an alternative to challenge the power and hierarchy of the existing order. This ideology may find out from the analysis of the language and linguistic settings of the Healing Discourse.

healed. The New Testament scholars identify this expression as very unique one in the healing discourse in which Jesus connects sin with healing. With the opening of this word Jesus affirms the qualitative content of discourse. In this expression Jesus' identify got a privileged position which is questioned in the later part by the scribes.

The Gospel of Mark situates Jesus in a hierarchical order in the beginning of the discourse. The writer or the community of the writers use the word or the whole ideology and religious ambiguities of the *ἁμαρτίαι (hamartiai).*[133] According to Critical Discourse Analysis, this is an important linguistic tool to identify the "production processes" in a discourse which Van Dijk's also proposed in his theory.[134] *ἁμαρτίαι (hamartiai)* functions as the key term which leads the discourse into the end production of the meaning. In contrast there were scribes who have had extremely different ideologies over *ἁμαρτίαι (hamartiai)* and the authority over *ἁμαρτίαι (hamartiai)*. Thus, the body of the paralysed had been presented or *χαλῶσι Chalosi,* meaning let down or lower in to the discourse of *ἁμαρτίαι (hamartiai)* and the authority for forgiving *ἁμαρτίαι (hamartiai)*. Therefore, the body is a social variable which carries the multiple aspects of the *ἁμαρτίαι (hamartiai)* and its socio-religious-political as well as the cultural understanding of the Greco-roman world.

4.2.2.2. Context of the Body

The word *μὴ δυνάμενοι (me dunamenoi)* meaning 'not being able' is important to be noticed in the discussion of the context of the body. The word throws light on the obstacles before the community who tries to reach to Jesus with the paralysed one. The linguistic function of the word is to portray the situation of restriction and

---

[133] According to the Jewish understanding only God has the authority to forgive sins. A miracle worker may heal a person but he cannot forgive his/her sins. Therefore this particular placing of Jesus as the authority to forgive sin is a counter statement in which the Gospel writer tried to establish the emergence of the new authority, Jesus.

[134] See chapter one section 4.2.

denial. The inability of the group who seek deliverance of the paralysed is clearly portrayed with that expression. The discourse zooms in at the possibility of the presence of the scribes whose interventions in the healing opens the existing disputes and ambiguities at the spot where the body is placed. Religion has been the cause of the dispute and positioning of scribes at the spot could be associated with the presence of the religious authorities. The task of the scribes was mentioned in the discourse with the word *διαλογιζόμενοι (dialogizomenoi),* meaning questioning. Moulton and Milligan note that the word always has the sense of "inward deliberation or questioning."[135] The word placed the whole ideology of the scribes and its critical position against the concerns of salvation through Jesus. The space of this questioning was καρδία (*Kardia),* meaning heart. In Hebraic thought the heart is at the centre of intellectual activity. Therefore, the context of the body is in the centre of conflict issues like sin and authority. Scribes in Verse 7 also projects the issue of blasphemy. βλασφημεῖ *(Blasphemei),* the verb in this passage contemplates God as the object of the blasphemy.[136] Thus the plot of the discourse can be aligned with three important factors: firstly, the issue of the conditioned crowd; secondly, the religious presence in the healing space as a questioning system; thirdly, the presentation of Jesus as New authority who overturns the existing system of thought with alternative order. Multiple ideologies form a conclave and conceive discourse within the ambits of the paralysed body. According to the Critical Discourse Analysis, language is a 'social act'[137] in which one can identify the play of society and its ideologies in every level. Thus, the healing discourse also reflects such social acts and ploys which have their own consequential stories.

---

[135] Robert G. Brathcher and Eugene A. Nida. *A Translator's Handbook on the Gospel of Mark* (Leiden: E.J Brill, 1961), 77.

[136] Robert G. Brathcher and Eugene A. Nida. *A Translator's Handbook on the Gospel of Mark,* 78.

[137] See chapter one.

4.2.3. Healing Discourse: Language and Power

The functioning of power in the discourse is one of the key analytical tasks of the critical discourse analysis. Michael Foucault states that Power is not an institution, and not a structure; neither is it a certain strength we are endowed with; it is the name that one attributes to a complex strategic situation in a particular society.[138] Therefore, the analysis demands a search in the functioning of power in the healing discourse. The healing discourses tried to establish Jesus as the centre figure and language played an important role in this establishment. In the first part of the healing discourse from verses 1 to 4 make a general setting which portrayed the hierarchy of Jesus. The reference of the 'crowd', 'not being able to reach', 'preaching' all are the specific phrases in which the Gospel writer presented Jesus as the centre of the Discourse. After the preliminary settings, from verse 5 the discourse distinguishes Jesus as the Authority. In order to do this the Gospel writer aims to construct an identity of power to Jesus in the healing discourse. The following are some of the important words and phrases by which power is established through the language.

ἀφίενταί σου αἱ ἁμαρτίαι (Aphientai sou hai hamatiai): This is one of the significant phrases in which the gospel writer portrayed Jesus' hierarchy. The meaning says that *your sins are forgiven.* It is important to note the linguistic significance of this phrase. The gospel writer employed the passive without defining the subject of the action of the verb 'forgive.'[139] The actualisation of the authority through the passive is the way power established to the identity of Jesus. Again in V 1, Jesus says, with reference to himself, 'the son of man has authority on Earth to forgive sins'. Both the title 'the son of man' and the qualifying phrase 'upon the earth' are significant. Both are true instances for the way language brings power over identities.

---

[138] Michael Foucault, *History of Sexuality*, vol.1, 93.

[139] Robert G. Brathcher and Eugene A. Nida. *A Translator's Handbook on the Gospel of Mark,* 76.

ἀφίημι (Aphiemi): It carries the meaning 'send forth' or 'go away' and the verb is used in Mark with three main meanings. Firstly, 'let allow' or 'permit.'[140] Secondly, 'forgive', 'remit'. 'Pardon.'[141] Thirdly, 'leave.'[142] All these meanings carry the sense of authority that permits someone to move forward. Jesus' power is the demonstrating factor in this framing and placing of the words.

Σοὶ λέγω *(Soil lego)*: 'to you I say', the order of the Greek makes the personal pronoun *soi 'to you'* emphatic and this portrayed the sense of command from the authority. This saying was placed after the encounter with the scribes and which may also emphasize the value of this saying as an authoritarian response over against the counter voices.

In all these words and phrases the analysis identifies the linguistic functioning of the words and phrases which creates power and hierarchy in order to establish the identity of Jesus beyond the existing social as well as the religious order of life. Gerd Theissen also tried to identify the Jesus' resistance against the framing of divine in to the boundaries of certain communities and territories.[143] The unspoken questions of the scribes and the reassuring response from Jesus makes it clear that Jesus wants to teach or let across his authority specifically his authority to forgive sins.[144] Language played an important role in this establishment. Therefore, the critical discourse analysis is true in stating that language is a tool to create power.

---

[140] See mark 1:34, 5:19,37, 7:12,27, 10:14, 11:6, 16, 15:36.

[141] See mark 2:5,7,9,10, 3:28, 4:12, 11:25.

[142] See mark 12:19,20,22, 13:2.

[143] Gerd Theissen, *The New Testament – History, Literature, Religion,* ed. Tr. John Bowden (New York: T &T Clark, 2003), 38.

[144] Tat – Siong Benny Liew. "The Gospel of Mark" in *A Postcolonial Commentary on the New Testament Writings,* ed. Fernando F. Segovia and R. S Sugirtharajah (New York: T&T Clark, 2007), 117.

4.2.4. Healed Body: Re-imagination of Alternatives

In the analysis one can identify the paralysed body acts as the crux of a social space in which the discourse emerged and developed its idea and meaning. The meaning of the discourse through the healed body of the paralysed has been established. The healed body should be viewed in terms of the product of the discourse. The healed body reflects the new identity offered by Jesus and this identity is an alternative identity received through Jesus. Jesus' identity revealed in this discourse is the identity of a New being and God. Through his entry into a reordering of power, Jesus is acting on God's behalf and fulfilling the commission that was bestowed on him at his baptism. A new aspect of Jesus' ministry is manifested here: a negation of sacred tradition, a reordering of the world and most significantly a resurrecting of reality in which the vertically or transcendence of the reality of God begins to express itself horizontally in and through the activity of a human being, a New Human being.[145] The author's final placing of the doxology in the discourse offered by the crowd is an attempt to make a universal claim for Jesus' authority. This is an alternative direction since the scribes mentioning of *one God* reflects the singularity of Israel's God.[146] The question rightly reflects the contemporary Jewish perception that the forgiveness of sins was exclusively God's prerogative. This was the consistent pattern of the Old Testament as well as the intertestamental Literature. The statement is formulated in the present passive. The passive is a periphrasis indicating divine action attributed as 'God forgives'. The present also indicates absolute certainty of God's forgiveness as an event happening now. The nearness of God's rule links healing and forgiveness.[147] Therefore, the portrayal of Jesus' proclamation of forgiveness of sin is an alternative idea of God, the authority and

---

[145] Herman C. Waetjen. *A Reordering of Power: A Socio-Political Reading of Mark's Gospel* (Minneapolis: Fortress Press,1989), 87.

[146] Robert A. Guelich. *World Biblical Commentary: Mark* 1-8:26 34A (Texas: Word Books Publishers,1989), 87.

[147] Herman Hendrickx. *The Miracle Stories: Studies in the Synoptic Gospels* (San Francisco: Harper & Row Publishers,1987), 121.

work of God. This is one of the significant meanings which the discourse yielded to.

4.3. Mark: 5:1-21: Text and Context

This event occurred in a gentile territory when Jesus and his disciples reach their destination on the eastern shore of the Sea of Galilee and began to enter the country of the Gerasenes. Geographically speaking the boundary of Gerasa and its surrounding countryside did not reach to the edge of the lake; the city itself is approximately thirty miles away from the sea. It is a narrative of the destruction of demonic powers of living death and dehumanization. The Greek term *δαιμόνιον* (*daimonion)* had a wide range of meaning.

4.3.1. Body and Social Location

4.3.1.1. Placing of Body

The body possessed by demonic powers was brought before Jesus as he entered the territory of the great provincial city of Gerasa on the border of the Roman Empire. In the very beginning of the discourse it placed the identity of the Empire which is important in the context. In the later part of the discourse also makes connections with the empire and the authority of the empire. The placement of the 'empire' in the discourse is placed in such a way that the discourse may consider as Jesus' encounter with the empire. The identity of the body was described as men with impure spirits who have come out of the tombs. Upon Jesus' alighting from the boat, a demoniac immediately appeared into view with terrifying, super natural swiftness and expressions. The confusion of identity between the demonic parasite and its human host is at once suggested by the phrase 'ἐκ τῶν μνημείων (*ek ton mnemeion)*', meaning 'out of the tomb'. Tomb is connected with the Greek understanding of Demons and their dwelling place. The placing of the word *μνημα* (*mnema)* directly lifts the discourse to the existing understandings and discourses on demons in the Greco-roman socio-political and religious space. The man's identity has been swallowed up by the demon's, so that he speaks with the demon's voice, tries to protect the demon from eviction from his own body and become the demon's instrument for his own torture.[148] He lived in a deserted, unclean place, among the graves, no one can chain him or tame him, and he spends night and day howling through the tombs and the hills and cutting himself with stones. The overall impression is of a person who has lost control of himself. Therefore, the placing of the body in this discourse put forth an issue of objectification.

Another important thing in connection with the placing of the body in this discourse is the geography. This is the first narrative in Jesus' public ministry in a Jewish region and it was a description of Exorcism. The maiden encounter of Jesus in a Jewish region was an encounter with the issue of daemons and exoticism. Therefore, the placing of the body happened in the discourse is significant because it happened as Jesus' primordial response to the Jewish social and religious space. The whole discourse made an attempt to address the concerns of empire through the demonic body. The body represents a wider context of the land and its knowledge. The issue of the demonic world understanding of the land and the issues of the empire goes hand in hand and the discourse tried to re-establish both knowledge systems through his alternative knowledge.

4.3.1.2. Context of the Body

The Greek term *δαιμόνιον* (*daimonion)* had a wide range of meaning but the negative aspects of the term got predominant acceptance in early Judaism for referring to hostile spirits. Demons' most direct attack on an individual was through possession. Various prophylactic methods were meant to ward off demonic attacks of diverse kinds, but in the case of possession a cure took the form of exorcism. Those who practise exorcism sometimes employed commands and Jesus also did the practice of exorcism. Even their

---

[148] Joel Marcus. *The Anchor Bible: Mark* 1-8 Vol. 27 (New York: Doubleday, 2000), 348.

commands usually belonged to a larger context of incantations and often accompanied various rituals.[149]

The Greek term translated demon not in itself is negative, and the meaning of the term evolved over time. It could refer to the spirits of the deceased, including prominent heroes of the past; it could involve good or ill fortune. It could denote a particular deity or even deity more generally. Greek often applied the term to deities like the Olympians, but more commonly to lower, super human spirits and demigods or deified mortals.[150] In middle Platonism, humans could become heroes, *δαιμόνιον* (*daimonion),* and finally divine; or the *δαιμόνιον* (*daimonion)* could also regress back into mortal bodies and eventually face death. They were intermediaries connecting and communicating between the divine and human realms. These intermediary spirits could be either good or bad; however, the semantic range includes a negative usage. In the later period the term could refer to an evil spirit.

The demons dwelled in different places like reed stalks, palm and other trees and some may found in ruins, in bath houses, in graveyards and elsewhere. Apparently they could not attack anyone in the holy city of Jerusalem. Some spirits may recognize God's sovereignty; God was sovereign over all spirits in the vast majority of early Jewish literary sources. Demons could also be arranged in ranks or legions. Therefore, the demon in this text should understand in the backdrops of these wide varieties of concepts and ideologies. In other words the body of the demon is a carrier of these demonic understandings of the Greco-Roman world. Thus, the discourse also needs to be seen as a discourse on demonic thought rather mere exoticism.

4.3.4. Healing Discourse: Language and Power

The work of language as a tool to establish power and hierarchy or Jesus is important to be noticed. The author's linguistic intentions

---

[149] Craig S. Keener. *Miracles: The Credibility of The New Testament Accounts* Vol. 1 (Grand Rapids: Baker Academics, 2011), 669-770.

[150] Craig S. Keener. *Miracles: The Credibility of The New Testament Accounts* Vol. 1, 771.

create the identity of Jesus as the new authority emerging in the Jewish land.

ἔδραμεν καὶ προσεκύνησεν αὐτῷ (Edramen Kai Prosekunesen auton): 'He ran and prostrated himself before him'. The expression portrayed the reverence when the man fell down before Jesus. *προσεκύνηο (Proskuneo)* opens the possibility of inferring the meaning as 'do reverence', 'make obeisance', 'bow down to', 'worship' etc. Here the possibility is to identify it as an act of reverence rather than worship. The placement of the words eventually elevates the identity of Jesus higher and place the demon lower to Jesus. *προσεκύνηο (Proskuneo)* also tries to represent the surrendering of the body before a naturally higher order. The description of the demon in verse 5 already set the foundation of the *προσεκύνηο (Proskuneo)* and the establishment of the hierarchy of Jesus. In verse 5 the demon was described as a powerful body so that 'no one can chain him or tame him'. Therefore, *προσεκύνηο (Proskuneo)* could be considered as the surrendering of this power which cannot be controlled by the existing powers or people. Linguistically and thematically the beginning of the discourse portrayed the strong man and in later part the discourse presented Jesus the ultimate power who overcomes the strong man and *προσεκύνηο (Proskuneo)* is functioning as the linguistic tool to develop this ideology.

ἔλεγεν γὰρ αὐτῷ (Elegen gar auto): Meaning is *for he was saying to him.* The imperfect indicates either that Jesus was in the act of exorcising the unclean spirit when interrupted by the demoniac or Jesus was repeating his command. The meaning of the verb *λεγο* (*lego)* 'say' here functioned as 'command', 'order'. One can identify the progress of Jesus' authority as the discourse gets progressed. In the beginning of the discourse the affirmation of Jesus' authority expressed through the demon and here Jesus himself expressed it through the command over the demon. The discourse portrayed this as Jesus' self declaration about his authority over the existing power.

παρεκάλει (Parekalei): Meaning is 'he begged'. Mark uses the imperfect, which indicates repeated or continuous action because these pleas are in vain and therefore repeated. In verse 12 the tense changed to the aorist because that plea is granted. This sort of linguistic placing show the continuing affirmation of Jesus' power and authority over the unclean spirit. This expression need not imply any fond attachment which the man had for the demons which possessed him, but he uttered this request as the spokesman for the demons. This also presents the status of the demonic power before Jesus. The discourse presents the identity of demons under the mercy of Jesus and it clearly states that the demons have no other options but to beg before Jesus. This portrayal leads to the declaration of Jesus' authority by the demonic powers. Therefore the word *παρεκάλει (Parekalei)* functions as a word which makes the continuity of the discourse on Jesus' authority over evil spirits.

***υἱὲ τοῦ θεοῦ τοῦ ὑψίστου (Huie ton theou tou hupsistou)*:** Meaning, *son of the most high God.* Here the discourse develops a Christological title to Jesus. The 'Most High God' in Old Testament and Jewish texts is associated not only with Gentiles but also with the sovereignty of the God of Israel over the whole earth, even gentile realms.[151] This title also reminisces of holy war in which this sovereignty has been established in the Old Testament history.[152] The casting out of legion of demons also affirms that the 'son of the Most High God' is subduing a hostile Gentile territory through a saving act of holy war.[153] The theme of God's holy war victory is also associated with the 'Most High God' title in 2 Sam 22:14. When we consider the geography in the discourse this title brings new meaning. The discourse tried to mark Jesus' identity suitable with the Jewish understanding of God as well. In a way the title suggests Jesus as the God of everyone both Gentiles and Jewish. The title proposes the universal nature of divinity in Jesus.

4.3.5. Healed Body: Re-imagination of Alternatives

It is a narrative of the destruction of demonic powers of living death and dehumanization.

---

[151] Joel Marcus. *The Anchor Bible: Mark* 1-8 Vol. 27, 344.

[152] See Gen 14:10; Psalms 9:3; 47:2, 83:18.

[153] Joel Marcus. *The Anchor Bible: Mark* 1-8 Vol. 27, 344.

Λεγιὼν (Legion) in 5:9 has a wider sociological value in this discourse. Werner Kelber suggests that *Λεγιὼν (Legion)* indicates a military and economic meaning that reflects a context of Roman – occupied territory and not the sociocultural milieu of Rome.[154] As a signifier the name *Λεγιὼν (Legion)* seems to bear several layers and levels of meaning. First, it is a Latin military term and links the demoniac to the institution of the Roman army. But, we need to analyse the intention of this symbolic way of narration in this discourse. Most likely it is an intention of colonialism. Through the economic exploitation, political suppression, its systematic denial of all attributes of humanity is to its subjugated people of colonialism creates an atmosphere of living death in human life situations. Therefore, *Λεγιὼν (Legion)* could be impressed upon as the representative of social control. Jesus' encounter with *Λεγιὼν (Legion)* was the declaration of freedom over the clutches of bondages. In a way the discourse produces the meaning of new life and freedom of self with Jesus. The healing constitutes a new creation, a victory over the rule of Satan.

The second alternative is with the healed body. He requested Jesus to allow him to join them but Jesus refused to take him along with him and he instructed him to return to home. He instructed him to remain in the same territory as a man who experiences the freedom of life. Jesus proposed a new model of discipleship without following him physically. He proposed a different order of life as an authority. As an authority the healed body is ever obliged to Jesus but Jesus used his power to offer ultimate freedom of identity. This alternative is very interesting in connection with power and hierarchy. Through all these alternatives Jesus offers the foretaste of Kingdom of God in which life is the celebration of ultimate freedom in God. The healing discourse righty establishes this alternative and produces a wider meaning.

---

[154] Herman C. Waetjen. *A Reordering of Power: A Socio-Political Reading of Mark's Gospel,* 13.

4.4. Mark: 10:46-52: Text and Context

This miracle is one of the most significant miracle discourses in Mark because other than exoticism the one miracle Jesus performed that is not recorded in the Hebrew scriptures is giving of sight to a blind man.[155] The incident involving the blind beggar, Bartimaeus, is the last of the healing miracles recorded by Mark. Jericho was the important geographical mentioning in this discourse. The first three Gospels make Jericho at the southern end of the River Jordan's deep valley, the final stop for Jesus on his way to Jerusalem for the climax of his life and ministry.[156] The religious authorities that the high priest, Caiaphas, had advised the Great Council that Jesus was great threat to national security and it would be best for all if he died. Jesus had tactfully withdrawn from the area. As the greatest of the three pilgrimage festivals approached, the combined feast of Passover and unleavened bread, Jesus decided that he must confront the authorities with his claim and force them to accept or reject him once for all. He and the disciples took the road to Jerusalem again and crossed the Jordan valley just north of the Dead Sea. As they were passing through Jericho a blind beggar called Bartimaeus shouted out and hailed Jesus as son of David. The presence of a blind beggar outside the city gates, on the pilgrimage way was a common scene in the Ancient West Asia. The preservation of his name is unusual, and is limited in the Marcan account. Mark gives both the Aramic and the Greek equivalent of the name. Mark very rarely records names in connection with incidents of healing that it is probable that the son of *Timai* was known in the later church.

---

[155] Ben Witherington III. *The Gospel of Mark: A Socio-Rhetorical Commentary* (Grand Rapids: William B. Eerdmans Publishing Company, 2001), 291.

[156] Joseph Rhymer. *The Miracles of Jesus* (United Kingdom: St Paul Publication, 1965), 66.

4.4.1. Body and Social Location

4.4.1.1. Placing of Body

The placing of the Body in this discourse was significant in many aspects. Firstly, the body was not an unknown body and the body has an identity. Only Mark gave the name of the person who was healed, and this is the only place where he did so. Secondly, the placing of the body at the entrance to Jericho also important to be noticed because this geographical location has religious significance. Jericho was located about five miles west of the Jordan and eighteen miles northeast of Jerusalem.[157] The name of the city also used to indicate that Jesus is near to Jerusalem and nearing to his goal.[158] This is one of the famous pilgrim routes where the pilgrims go to Jerusalem for the feast.[159] Thirdly, though the presence of a blind beggar just outside the city gates, on the pilgrimage way was a common scene the discourse tried to place the identity of this beggar higher than a mere beggar. The presentation of the beggar with a name and his recognition of Jesus in a very significant expression as 'Son of David' also raise the value of his identity from a mere beggar. It carries a bearing that prior to his entry to Jerusalem Jesus was called as 'son of David'. This may also be the end of messianic secret as the passion draws near, when Jesus will be fully revealed of his identity. All these conceptual and literary settings of the presentation of the body portrayed the socio-religious settings for Jesus' entry to Jerusalem.

4.4.1.2. Context of the Body

Healing of blindness has long been considered significant and appears in some ancient, extra biblical miracle claims. Ancients

---

[157] William L. Lane. *The Gospel of Mark: The New International Commentary on the New Testament* (Grand Rapid: William B, Eerdmans Publishing Company, 1974), 387.

[158] Ben Witherington III. *The Gospel of Mark: A Socio-Rhetorical Commentary,* 291.

[159] See Psalms 42:4.

frequently believed that, under extra ordinary circumstances, blind persons could be supernaturally healed.[160] Jesus movement also connected with healing of blind people. These healing episodes may be found in Gospel narrations.[161] As it was mentioned above the presence of a blind beggar just outside the city gates, on the pilgrimage way was a common scene. Therefore, the context is familiar and more natural in terms of its cause. Another familiarity in the context of the body is related to the messianic secret. There was an existing understanding which Isaiah also mentioned that when the messiah came, he would cure the blind. The messianic thought and its connection to the healing of blind is also part of the context of the body.

4.4.2. Healing Discourse: Language and Power

***Υἱὲ Δαυὶδ (Huie David)*:** meaning *'Son of David'.* The announcement of this title has very significant role in the whole discourse. The placing of this title may consider as the expression in which the messianic secret ends before Jesus' entry to Jerusalem. The identity of Jesus is the question emerged from the context. The continuing debate of Jesus' identity as messiah, magic worker, zealot, prophet etc., reaches in to the climax. The writer of the Mark Gospel tried to reveal his identity so clear with another healing Discourse. The mentioning of the crowd in this context is also remarkable because they are the pilgrims going towards Jerusalem. Therefore, the placing of the title *'Son of David'* is functioning as the key to the purpose of Jesus' life as he enters into the city of Jerusalem. Mark tried to state the identity and authority of Jesus' yet again more specific and placed in an entirely different context. The 'son of David' title is commonly served as a synonym for 'the Messiah'.

***στὰς (stas)*:** Only here in Mark is στὰς used with the meaning 'standing still'. This word was used immediately after

---

[160] Craig S. Keener. *Miracles: The Credibility of The New Testament Accounts* Vol. 1, 511.

[161] See mark 8:22-26; 10:46-52, Matthew 11:5, Luke 7:22, John 9:7, Matthew 12:22, 15:30-31.

the mentioning of the crowds response on beggar. The narrator portrayed Jesus as a determined figure who never moved with ambitions of the external forces. 'Standing still' is very particular in order to bring out this identifies in Jesus. The continuity of this determination may identify in the temple of Jerusalem as well. This word functioned as a marker in which Jesus' identity is distinct from the 'Crowd'.

***ἡ πίστις σου σέσωκέν σε (He pistis sou sesoken)*:** This is another expression in which mark tried to raise the identity of Jesus from mere miracle worker and taking closer to the ultimate power of God. *σου (Sozo)* also may identify as 'saved'. This saving aspect is very important and which actually place Jesus' identity above other miracle workers of the time. The 'Saved' can refer to physical healing and spiritual healing, the gift of salvation. The extension of the saving may identify with the following mentioning *ἠκολούθει ekolouthei* express his following. The proclamation of 'saved' also shows the authority of Jesus because 'saving' act belongs to God alone and the discourse tried to develop Jesus' identity in to this level of greatness. This mentioning has very significant role in the pre-Jerusalem entry context.

***ἐν τῇ ὁδῷ (En te hoto)*:** meaning 'on the way'. The placing of the 'way' has symbolic meaning in this context. Jesus is on the way to the cross and the healed body is also following him on this 'way'. The narration presents the emerging followers of Jesus on his way to Jerusalem. The number of followers is not limited with twelve disciples. There are many like Bartimaeus following Jesus secretly. The development of Jesus' identity as a powerful and attractive figure is portrayed in this discourse. The climax of the discourse ends with this silent follower.

4.4.3 Healed Body: Re-imagination of Alternatives

This healing discourse tried to make some alternative ideas especially in the pre-Jerusalem entry of Jesus. The purpose of the discourse is to create a final declaration of Jesus' identity. The disclosure of messianic secret and the silence of Jesus against this messianic claim are very important in the pre-Jerusalem context.

The arrival of the new vision in Jesus is the prime alternative which this discourse tries to bring out. The healed body is the presented as the follower of this new vision which moves towards Jerusalem. Mark in this climax episode of healing discourses tried to present Jesus as the alternative power and authority going toward Jerusalem for change and restoration. The alternative is ultimately cross that we can find in the end of the narratives. The follower is also a significant marker which represents the alternative community which follows the way of Jesus to Jerusalem and beyond. The announcement of the identity is also considered as the announcement of the Kingdom of God which offered the new religious and political identity to Jesus and his followers.[162] The proposal a new community is the significant alternative which this discourse produces.

---

[162] C.I. David Joy, "Decolonizing the Bible, Church, And Jesus" in *Decolonizing the Body of Christ: Theology and Theory after Empire* ed. David Joy and Joseph Duggan (New York: Palgrave macmillan, 2012), 18.

Conclusion

The Critical Discourse Analysis of the Select Healing Stories in the Gospel of Mark tried to study the healing discourses as literary device in which the writer develop and create new meaning and alternative knowledge. Chapter one of the book made an attempt to present a critical overview of the methodology of CDS theory. Chapter two which focused on the Geo-political context of the Gospel of Mark, made an attempt to present major Socio-political, cultural and religious concerns of the time and connect it with the Gospel narrations. In the third chapter the overview of healing stories and its historical relevance in the primitive Christian faith and practice was presented. The chapter also analysed the importance of healing stories as social discourse by incorporating social scientific theories. The fourth chapter analyzed three healing discourses in the Gospel of Mark and critically analysed it with the methodological frame of CDS. This chapter also made an attempt to analyse linguistic approaches of the healing discourse to identify the production of the discourse.

The Marken healing discourses are the products of the person and actions of Jesus and their interest centres in their theological rather than in their historical characters. The healing discourse functioned as a literary tool in order to produce the meaning of new life and freedom of self of the communities with Jesus. The healing constitutes a new creation, a victory over the rule of evil and all the forces that create control and legitimisation. The healed body in the discourse represented the new community and new life in Jesus, the ultimate authority of life (§ 4.2.4, 4.3.5, 4.4.3). The Body of the diseased in the healing discourses represented the multiple contexts of the existing system of thought. Jesus' act in the healing discourses tried to address this systemic way of legitimisation of human body and identities. The problematization of the body is a symbolic encounter with the existing socio-political world views (§ 4.2.2.2, 4.3.3.2, 4.4.1.2). The deceased body in the healing discourses transcends the anthropological boundaries and functioned as the symbolic representation of Multiple Socio-religious, Political and Religious Context of the Greco-Roman world. (§ 4.2.2.1, 4.3.3.1, 4.4.1.1). The language and linguistics aspects in the healing Discourse played an important role in forming the healing discourse as Socio-Political Discourse of the time. The language and linguistic variants are the elements which carries the ideological intention of the discourses, to establish the authority of Jesus above every existing understanding of God in the Greco-Roman world (§ 4.2.3, 4.3.4, 4.4.2). The Discourse nature of the healing stories is a rhetoric tool in which the identity of Jesus got the hierarchical status. This hierarchical setting is an important element in making the distinctive nature and identity of Jesus (§ 4.2.4, 4.3.5, 4.4.3). The healing Discourses are the 'God talk' of the Greco-Roman socio-religious world. The ambiguities and contradictions on messiah, saviour, new being are the major contents of the God talk in the healing Discourses. The discourse tried to mark Jesus' identity suitable with the Jewish understanding of God as well. The healing discourse tries to propose the universal nature of divinity in Jesus. It suggests the idea that Jesus as the God of everyone both Gentiles and Jewish (§ 4.2.4, 4.3.5, 4.4.3). The healing Discourses are the theological alternatives of Jesus movement. Every healing Discourse proposed an alternative for the existing God – Man/Woman, Man/Woman – World relationship in this world. Through all these alternatives Jesus offers the foretaste of Kingdom of God in which life is the celebration of ultimate freedom in God (§ 4.2.4, 4.3.5, 4.4.3). The healing discourse functions as tool to portrayed Jesus' self declaration about his authority over the existing power. Jesus was presented as the most powerful and ultimate authority over every existing power order. The healing discourses denied this power order and develop an alternative order of life in Jesus. The victory over evil, scribes, and legion all portrayed his identity which surpasses all existing and domination powers of the World (§ 3.3, 5.3).

The outcome of this research also opens new horizons and wider scope for future directions of this methodological approach. The further researches could be helpful in reading the healing discourses as an ideological paradigm of the Gospel narrations and its implications in the Christological expressions of the Gospels. This methodological approach will further engage to study healing Discourses in order to opens new pathways for understanding the Jesus movement and the identity of Jesus though a socio - scientific perspective. The future research can also mark the issues of power and hierarchy in the Gospel narrations and in the presentation of Divine.

Bibliography

Bell, Allen and P. Garrett. *Approches to Media Discourse.* UK: Wiley-Blackwell, 1998.

Brathcher, Robert G. and Eugene A. Nida. *A Translator's Handbook on the Gospel of Mark.* Leiden: E. J. Brill, 1961.

Chancey, Mark A. *The Myth of a Gentile Galilee.* New York: Cambridge University Press, 2002.

Chouliaraki, Lilie and Norman Fairclough. *Discourse in Late Modernity–Rethinking Critical Discourse Analysis.* Edinburgh: Edinburgh University Press,1999.

Clark, K. W. "Galilee," *George A. Buttrick, The Interpreter's Dictionary of the Bible,* Vol. 2. New York: Abingdon Press, 1972.

Connor, Steven (ed.), *The Cambridge Companion to Postmodernism.* UK: Cambridge University Press, 2004.

David Joy, C. I. *Mark and its Subalterns: A Hermeneutical Paradigm for a Post Colonial Context.* London: Equinox, 2008.

__________. "Decolonizing the Bible, Church, and Jesus" in *Decolonizing the Body of Christ: Theology and Theory after*

Empire ed. David Joy and Joseph Duggan (New York: Palgrave Macmillan, 2012.

Davies, Stevan L. *Jesus the Healer. London*: SCM Press, 1995.

Eve, Eric. *The Healer from Nazareth: Jesus Miracles in Historical Context.* London: SPCK, 2009.

Fairclough, Norman. *Discourse and Social Change.* Cambridge: Polity Press,1992.

__________. *Critical Discourse Analysis*. Boston: Addison Wesley, 1995.

Foucault, Michel. *Discipline and Punish.* New York: Vintage Book, 1979.

__________. *History of Sexuality,* Vol.1. New York: Random House, 1990.

__________. *Power*, ed. James D. Faubion USA: New Press, 1994.

Fower, Roger. *Language and Control*. London: Routledge, 1979.

__________. *Literature as Social Discourse: The Practice of Linguistic Criticism.* USA: Indiana University Press, 1981.

Grant, Robert M. *Miracle and Natural Law in Greco-Roman and Early Christian Thought*. Amsterdam: Noord-hollandsche Uitgevers – Maatschapij, 1952.

Guelich, Robert A. *World Biblical Commentary: Mark 1-8:26 34A*. Texas: Word Books Publishers, 1989.

Hare, Douglas R. *Mark.* Louisville: Westminster John Knox Press, 1996.

Hendrickx, Herman. *The Miracle Stories: Studies in the Synoptic Gospels*. San Francisco: Harper & Row Publishers, 1987.

Hengel, Martin. *The "Hellenizatio" of Judaea in the First Century After Christ.* London: SCM Press, 1989.

Hodge R. & G Kress. *Social Semiotics*. Cambridge: Polity Press, 1988.

Jeremias, Joachim. *Jerusalem In the Time of Jesus.* Philadelphia: Fortress Press, 1969.

Kee, Howard Clark. *Medicine, Miracle and Magic in New Testament Times.* Cambridge: Cambridge University Press, 1986.

Keener, Craig S. *Miracles: The Credibility of The New Testament Accounts Vol 1.* Grand Rapids: Baker Academics, 2011.

Lane, William L. *The Gospel of Mark: The New International Commentary on the New Testament.* Grand Rapid: William B, Eerdmans Publishing Company, 1974.

Laverdiere, Eugene. *The Beginning of the Gospel: Introducing the Gospel According to Mark.* Minnesota: The Liturgical Press, 1991.

Liew, Tat – Siong Benny . *'The Gospel of Mark' in A Postcolonial Commentary on the New Testament Writings,* Fernando F. Segovia and R. S Sugirtharajah (Ed.). New York: T&T Clark, 2007.

Locke, Terry. *Critical Discourse Analysis.* New York: Continuum, 2004.

Lott, Eric J. *Healing Wings: Acts of Jesus for Human Wholeness.* Bangalore: Asian Trading Corporation, 1998.

Louw, J. P. "Reading a Text as Discourse," in Linguistics and New Testament Interpretation: Essays on Discourse Analysis ed. D. A. Black. Nashville: Broadman, 1992.

Marcus, Joel. *The Anchor Bible: Mark 1-8 Vol. 27.* New York: Doubleday, 2000.

Murphy, Frederick J. *The Religious World of Jesus.* Nashville: Abingdon Press, 1991.

Murphy., Frederick J. *The Religious World of Jesus.* Nashville: Abingdon Press, 1991.

O'Farrell, Clare. *Michel Foucault.* New Delhi: Sage Publication, 2005.

Rhymer, Joseph. *The Miracles of Jesus.* United Kingdom: St Paul Publication, 1965.

Richardson, Alan. *The Miracle Stories of The Gospel.* London: SCM, 1963.

Rivkin, Ellis. *A Hidden Revolution: The Pharisees' Search for the Kingdom within.* Nashville: Abingdon, 1978. Stemberger, Gunter. Jewish Contemporaries of Jesus: Pharisees, Sadducees, Essenes. Minneapolis: Fortress Press, 1995.

Roetzel, Calvin J. *The World that Shaped the New Testament.* Atlanta: John Knox Press, 1973.

Sarup, M. *An Introductory Guide to Post-structuralism and Postmodernism.* New York: Harvester Wheatsheaf, 1993.

Smart, Barry. *Michel Foucault.* London: Routledge Press, 2002.

Stanton, Graham. '*Message and Miracles*', *in Markus Bockmuehl* (ed.), The Cambridge Companion of Jesus. Cambridge: Cambridge University Press, 2001.

Stein, Robert H. *Mark: Baker Exegetical Commentary on the New Testament.* Grand Rapids: Baker Academic, 2008.

Theissen, Gerd. *The Miracle Stories of the Early Christian Tradition.* Edinburgh: T&T Clark, 1983.

__________. *The New Testament – History, Literature, Religion,* ed. Tr. John Bowden. New York: T & T Clark, 2003.

Twelftree, Graham H. *Jesus the Miracle Worker: A Historical and Theological Study.* Downers Grove, IL: InterVarsity Press, 1999.

Van Dijk, Teun A. *Discourse and Power.* New York: Palgrave Macmillan, 2008.

__________. *Handbook of Discourse Analysis. 4 Vols.* London: Academic Press, 1985.

Varkey, Mothy. *Concept of Power in Sermon on the Mount.* Tiruvalla: CSS, 2010.

Vermes, Geza. *Jesus the Jew.* (London: William Collins Sons, 1977), p. 46.

Waetjen, Herman C. *A Reordering of Power: A socio-Political Reading of Mark's Gospel.* Minneapolis: Fortress Press, 1975.

Witherington III, Ben. *The Gospel of Mark: A socio-Rhetoric Commentary.* Grand Rapids: William B. Eerdmans Publishing Company, 2001.

Wodak, Ruth &. Ludwig, *Challenges in a Changing World.* Vienna: Passagen Verlag, 1999.

Wodak, Ruth. *Disorders of Discourse.* London: Longman, 1995.

Journal

Peterson, Norman R. "'Point of View' in Mark's Narrative", in Semeia 12 (1978): 97-121.